BEing Spiritually Intelligent

VOLUME I

The Missing Link Between
Who You Are
&
Who You Were Meant to BE

Susan Abrams Milligan

Published by:
Bright Eyes Network LLC
2370 SR 89A, Ste 11-414
Sedona, AZ 86336

This book is to be regarded as a reference source and is not
intended to replace professional medical advice or prescribe
the use of any technique as a form of treatment for physical,
emotional, or medical problems without the advice of your
physician. The author and the publisher disclaim any liability
arising directly or indirectly from the use of this book.

ISBN: 978-0-9887207-0-1

Cover design: Myss Miranda
Editing: Jamie Lynn Sands
Printed in the United States of America

ACKNOWLEDGEMENTS

This book may never have been written, if it had not been for the many people who have influenced me. In this way, I have come to know who I really am. There have literally been thousands of people that I have met along the way who have become not only my teachers and mentors, but also my dear friends. It would be impossible to list them all here.

If I have ever met you, just know that even though you may not be personally listed, that you in some way, had a part in creating this book.

My husband and best friend,
Michael Milligan
My parents,
Gilbert and Elizabeth Abrams
Brother, James (Jim) Abrams,
who taught me more by his passing,
than if he had stayed
on this earth plane.

Sisters, Linda Warrick and Kathleen Biggins
All of our past and present pets

All of my relatives, friends, and coworkers
My clients, coaches and business mentors

My spiritual teachers:
Dr. Wayne Dyer, Louise Hay,
Marianne Williamson, Alan Cohen,
Marcia Wiener,
Dr. Robert Holden, Eckert Tolle,
Esther and Jerry Hicks, Abraham,
Gregg Braden,
John Holland, Sandi Phillips,
Koelle Simpson, James Redfield,
Klemmer & Associates,
The Heart Math Institute,
and especially,
Neale Donald Walsch.

Your collective consciousness has produced this book. I forever honor you and send you Love and Light for the grace you exchanged with me. It has lifted me up and touched my spirit.

❤ ❤ ❤

CONTENTS

INTRODUCTION

If someone had sat me down and told me forty years ago what I am about to share with you, my life would have been quite different. It is my hope that this book not only helps you discover who you really are earlier than I did, but also guides you to recreate yourself with the power you were born with.

This book was written in segments and stored in my head over many years of my life, although I knew it would eventually be a complete book and possibly more than one. Neale Donald Walsch, best selling author of the series, *"Conversations with God,"* encouraged me to seriously focus and to deliberately go through the process of writing the book every day. That process took me through a transformation, beyond what I ever expected. After discussing with Neale what I wanted to say and my apprehension over publicly saying it, he expertly suggested the final book title and subtitle. This is how it all began to take form.

Everyone has a number of books buried inside struggling to come out. The very act of transferring our deepest thoughts and sense of knowingness onto paper solidifies its ability to transform into a physical reality. Putting this information either on an online blog and/or into book form, are the best ways to share what we have learned in our short time on this earth. Generations to come will then benefit from our experiences.

We do not need to be a genius to put our thoughts on paper. We are each writing a book in our own head every single minute of our lives. Let's suppose we were capable of typing up our every thought every minute of every day; there would be an amazing amount of information stored for those who come after us. The question then is, what would be the main focus and title of each chapter in your book? Would it be an uplifting, feel-good book, or would it be a horror story, drama, or mystery? Perhaps it would be a little of all.

Does that idea make you cringe? Do you think no one would care? I'd suggest that you take a moment to reconsider. You may be surprised to find that more people care than you may have imagined. Would helping one person get through whatever they are facing, simply by reading a book based on your thoughts, make it all worthwhile? Is your answer still no? What if that one person was YOU?

Writing our thoughts down helps us to sift through the irrelevant clutter of life. In this way, we can stay focused on what is important. A mentor once told me, "Design your life around what matters most." This means that in order to do so, I will need to define in writing what kind of life I want. What would it look like? How would I feel living it? Who else would it help? How could I share it with others? Above all, how would my sense of "BEing" be strengthened so that I have a higher awareness of others and myself? If this sounds New Age to you, give it little thought beyond

this page. Those who refer to New Age as something negative do not understand what it is. The definition will depend on who is interpreting it, because there are as many different definitions as there are people who attempt to define it.

To be able to know and love others fully, including those who have different viewpoints, we must first know and love ourselves. BEing Spiritually Intelligent is about combining a wholesome body, mind, emotion, and spirit (with much emphasis on emotion and spirit), so that we feel at peace and fully in the state of joy. This will look differently for each person and it is a continual process of personal mastery. The important thing to know is that everyone is doing their best in life with the information that they have at any particular space in time in order to survive. The objective of this book is to help bridge the gap or to be the catalyst that empowers us to remove fear from our lives, including and most importantly, the fear of OURSELVES.

My Haunting

When seeing or hearing the word "haunting," most people picture in their minds something with evil connotations. For this reason, I was hesitant to use the term to describe the distressing persistence I felt over the years to get these thoughts and feelings on paper. I decided to use the word anyway, calling this a "haunting," because that is exactly what it felt like. However, this persistent calling relentlessly reminded me frequently and so intensely, that it could no longer be ignored or pushed to the back burner of my to-do list. It became a sense of knowing that the time for this book was now, from a deeper level than my intellectual mind.

Therefore, I would have to say that I have been haunted by spirit for over twenty years. What I mean by a "haunting," is that God, Spirit, the Universe, or whatever your truth calls the Divine, has been intensely calling me to share the message through this book.

However, I still resisted. Spirit calls us subtly at first. When we do not listen, it becomes stronger until we are willing to create a shift that is for our highest good.

In a matter of minutes I chose to stop resisting and move forward through my book. Sadly, there are many others who are looking for their voice to be heard. They too, for whatever reasons, have resisted writing, producing a movie, blogging, or whatever it is that would help them to articulate and live the truth of who they really are.

When others see how happy we are, living and BEing in our truth, they will be inspired to do the same. It is especially appealing to them when they see that we are passionate about doing what we love, on a much deeper level than ever before. We cannot make choices for other people. As much as we would like to help everyone, there are some people who simply don't realize they are unhappy. It is just where they are at this particular time in their life. When they do come into full realization, they must then accept that it is so, and be willing to take the necessary steps to make changes. All we can do for them is to be the example. By BEing Spiritually Intelligent and leading by example, everyone who is ready to follow our lead – will – and with Divine Intention for the greater good.

My in-depth quest for spiritual information and understanding also began over twenty years ago. Not only did I have a hunger to study, learn, and grow through spiritual development, I have also made it my mission to study extensively in the areas of: personal, emotional, leadership, and business development, as well as touching on science, philosophy, and physics. While on this path, I realized that many people do not pursue their own truth, because they fear knowing. On some level they also understand that once they do, they cannot un-know it. To admit this knowledge to themselves would change all or most of their current belief systems about life. For others, it is simply that they do not know there is a bigger picture to consider.

The purpose of this book is not to tell you about my experiences or all that I have studied over the years. It is to share with you HOW what I have studied has affected me permanently through my experience of it. More importantly, the purpose is to let you know that it has the potential to forever change your life as well.

The very fact that you are reading this book is not a coincidence. You were drawn to it because God, Spirit, the Universe, or by whatever name you choose as your Higher Power, is calling you to expand yourself beyond what you know, or believe you currently know about who you are and why you are here. I want to discuss the word "coincidence," so we are on the same page from the beginning. I use this word sparingly. In my heart, it is a slang word with a misinterpreted definition applied. Coincidence to most people means an uncanny or accidental occurrence of one or more events. The root word of coincidence is "coincide." The word, "coincide," means to occupy the same relative position or the same area in space; to happen at the same time or during the same period; and to correspond exactly, or be identical. There is definitely nothing accidental about the word "coincidence."

Would it surprise you to know that there are no coincidences? Everything happens for a reason, in perfect timing, and in Divine right order. When we begin to live our lives by accepting this truth, we do not have to move through life attempting to control, force, manipulate, or resist. It's the process of letting go that allows balance and flow to enter our lives. Note that I am not talking about floating through life without intentionally being the co-creator of what we experience. This is quite different, which you will read more about in a later chapter.

The continual flow of information through me has at times been so intense that it has affected my sleep patterns and overall self-care. If this is happening to you too, it may be your calling and your purpose to start forming into the physical world your book, blog, film, lyrics, poetry, art, song, music, etc. or whatever you are being called to do.

If you choose to continue to ignore it like I did, that's fine. It is always your choice as to when you make the shift, and may simply mean you are not yet ready. You will know when the time is right. There will continue to be countless opportunities, until you finally accept one of them. Keep in mind though, that when we resist something, it persists.

Throughout the years, I have likely read over a thousand books and attended hundreds of workshops. I began to wonder why they now seemed not to be as effective as I had previously found them. The reason was not because I knew it all, or that it wasn't the material I needed. It was because it was time to stop so much reading and attending workshops. It was time to start teaching and sharing the lessons and experiences I had learned over the many years. Spirit had been showing me that the best way to do this was through my own books and workshops. It took me a long time to reach that point, because like so many other people, I was in a space of resistance.

Here is another little pearl of wisdom. When you are resisting, you cannot CREATE. It is my hope that this book will help you, the reader, step into your own God-given power, while I also continue my own journey. We are all teachers and students at the same time.

While attending those workshops, sometimes with high profile spiritual teachers, I observed how they managed themselves along with the different challenges that other people presented them. I realized I was being drawn to this in order to prepare myself for what I was feeling called to do. I saw that they were just as human as I; they simply had more experience, but only because I had resisted stepping into spiritual teaching on a larger scale for so long.

HOW to move forward is not an issue when you stop resisting and have a passion for what you do, or what is sometimes referred to as a powerful "WHY." I call this process putting passion behind the action. When it is your calling, you will know it from a heart level of BEingness. By stepping into your truth, you are sharing with people who you really are. This gives them permission to do the same on a much deeper, more personal, and continual growth level. It's a process that becomes contagious.

It is simply your reminder of "who" you are, why you are here and it gives you back your power to make happen whatever you choose to be your reality. You create what you think about. The question is, "What are you thinking?"

This book was written through me, not by me. It was important to me that I wrote from the heart to those who resonate right now with its entirety or any portion of it. It was also written as a promise to self, God, and the universe, that I will do for others, what the contents of this book have done for me.

I pledge to be their platform, to be given the opportunity to be heard in whatever creative way they choose as their truth. I pledge to do my very best to keep EGO ("<u>E</u>dging <u>G</u>od <u>O</u>ut," as coined by Dr. Wayne Dyer) out of it. Again, because we are all both teacher and student at the same time, I realize that every person I encounter in my life teaches me something, provided I step outside of my EGO and choose to connect.

When you are ready to begin truly living your life with passion and greatness, turn the page and "allow" the next phase of your life to begin.

❤ ❤ ❤

.

1

BEING–SPIRITUALLY–INTELLIGENT

First, let's break each word down and get clear about what we want to collectively create. It is my intention that this book will be a bridge for you the reader, to use as a catalyst to empower you to let go of what is not serving you. By now, you are realizing that we have been living in a world that is not what we wanted it to be. You may be feeling that life is happening to you.

Do you truly understand how incredibly powerful you are? Every day you create worlds through your thoughts, choices, and actions: physical and non-physical. Did you know that? Did you know that it is not the fear of failure that holds you back? It is the fear of success. Understand that you cannot fail. It is impossible. Life is not happening to you, but rather, it is happening through you.

1. BEing -- Let's examine the word "BEing". The root of the word is "BE". Many people think that in order for them to have what they want, they have to <u>do</u> certain things, so they can <u>have</u> certain things, so that they can <u>BE</u> a certain way. However, as one of my spiritual mentors has stated, "What if everything we thought was wrong was actually right, and what we thought was right, was actually wrong?"

The message here is to pay closer attention, and to change our perspective about what is not serving us. There are an infinite number of choices we can make in every second of our lives. What we choose will create our experience.

When you are BEing a certain way and are in your heart space, you are living your life for the greater good of all. I call this Divine Intention. This is because you want everyone to WIN by having a positive life experience, and therefore, feel as good as you do. When this is your intent, with not a single person left out, you are BEing. You are now at peace, grounded, calm, and vibrating at a higher frequency of light energy. We will explore more on light energy in other chapters.

Throughout this book and most everything I now write, I capitalize BE when I mean the place of the heart – BEingness. This is not a typographical error. It is a mechanism to remind myself to BE in this state. That way, I am more fully aware and continually practice the evolution of BEing Spiritually Intelligent. I suggest that you, too, start this mind-to-heart shift as well by capitalizing BE when appropriate.

2. Spiritually -- The root word of spiritually is "spirit." The word spirit means different things to different people. It is your perspective that creates your definition, and there are an infinite number of perspectives. For the purpose of the content herein, I am defining it as something that is "greater than us, but also resides within us," because it exists everywhere.

Let's use the analogy of God, Universe, Higher Intelligence, Creator, (or whatever reference you use) as symbolically being the ocean. As the Bible and many other ancient holy books state, we are made in God's image and likeness. If we were to dip a thimble into the ocean (God), than we would become a thimble full of God. You may ask, "If spirit is symbolized by water, of what significance is the thimble?" The thimble (the biological body) is the container that holds the water (the spirit). Therefore, we are not human beings but Divine beings of light energy choosing to have a human experience.

When you look at God from that perspective, you know that there is something much bigger than anything we can individually create. We co-create it with spirit.

With all due respect, allow me to state that which is not spirituality. Spirituality is not a religion, although many people who are unaware of what it truly is often confuse the facts. Stating that spirituality is a religion is like stating that science, physics, geometry, mathematics, psychology, philosophy, heart coherent leadership, and personal development are also religions. Spirituality as you will soon learn, is the balanced marriage and interlacing of all of these combined plus more.

3. Intelligent -- We all know that the word intelligent is often a characteristic used to describe someone who is intellectually smart. You may have noticed over the last twenty years or more that there have been many references made to one's emotional intelligence. Wayne Payne coined the term in 1985, but Daniel Goleman created a pivotal point on the concept in the late 1990s when he published his popular book, "*Emotional Intelligence.*" It went viral in a positive way through the business world. His book focused mainly on interpersonal communications. It was indeed, a wake up call that spread like wildfire, because it was certainly needed by the business world at the time.

BEing Spiritually Intelligent does not have boundaries or limitations. It is a continual inner self-improvement process for each of us and does not stop at simply being emotionally smart. In other words, it does not stop at how well we communicate with others, how socially accepted we are within a group, or how we react to situations that do not serve us or others.

BEing Spiritually Intelligent includes:

- Recognizing without judging what is going on within YOU by BEing aware of your emotions.
- Taking personal response-ability for making changes when an emotion is not serving you or others.
- Deliberately creating the emotion you desire to raise your energy frequency.
- BEing authentic by respecting yourself and living the highest version of you with Divine Intention for all.

It includes and interlaces with emotional intelligence on a much grander scale. Nothing is more important than how you feel at all times. Reference the chapter, "Your Emotions Always Have and Always Will Matter."

Let your emotions BE your guide. Emotions are our natural internal radar as to whether something is serving us at the heart level, or if it is taking us farther away from our heart's wisdom. Notice the way you feel about any specific situation, person, environment, family, friend, or even a simple item you buy in the store. These feelings are all highly important to your overall well-BEing. When you get this fact and continually practice it, you will change your life -- permanently.

Your emotions in every second of every day will immediately let you know if something is not right, or something is very right. *"BEing Spiritually Intelligent"* is the marriage of all three of these components. We will go much deeper into many topics, which will relate back to all three of these words, individually, and collectively. We will also explore how to determine the difference between an emotion that is based on a FEAR that was triggered by something that happened in the past or an emotion from your natural internal radar system.

If finally understanding who you really are is of importance to you, you are going to love the next chapter.

❤ ❤ ❤

2

ALL LIFE IS A CIRCLE
IN MOTION

Think about the title of this chapter on a deeper level. Everything in life, including our solar system, universe, and any type of energy, including atoms, are circular and in motion at all times. Even the seasons of the earth and life itself are life-energy in motion.

Check any physics textbook and you will find scientific proof that absolutely everything is energy, even that which appears solid. This means that your front door, your dog, trees in your backyard, and clouds; all of it is energy, but in different forms. Even the process by which you think and dream are yet another form of energy. All energy vibrates.

Since everything is energy, let's consider the circular cycle of water. Snow and dew are water that has changed form. When water evaporates, where does it go? It is absorbed into the atmosphere and comes back to us in another form. Our thoughts and dreams are also a form of energy that we cannot physically see, because they are vibrating at a non-physical frequency.

Where do our thoughts and dreams go? For that matter, where do they come from? Let's explore this a little further. Would you judge snow or dew to be bad or wrong? Sure you have personal preferences but are either one truly wrong?

Our Physical Body, Our Light Body

Perhaps you have heard the quote, "We are a spiritual being having a human experience." Have we really thought about what those words mean on a much deeper level? It is an entertaining statement when thought about superficially. Quite possibly, it may touch our hearts, because we know there is some truth to it. However, when we begin to live our lives as this BEing true, the process of life begins to take on a whole new level or dimension of fun.

Our physical body is like a uniform. It is what we decided to wear while experiencing what we chose to experience here. That is, before we came onto this physical plane. What if we looked at our physical body as simply an outfit we chose to put on that day? How would that change our thoughts about who we thought we were?

Every morning when we wake up, we choose the clothing we are going to wear that day. The same thing occurs when we decide to awaken into this physical world (being conceived by our parents). Not only are we choosing our physical characteristics, such as our hair and eye color, the length of our fingers and toes, but we also decide what we want to experience in this life. Most importantly, we choose what challenges we want to experience and what triumphs we expect to come from those challenges.

Fast forward to this physical life we are experiencing now. On a moment-to-moment basis, we choose how often we will experience the same type of challenges, and to what degree those challenges will cause physical, emotional, or mental pain. We even decide the length of time to experience it before we break through into joy and enlightened awareness.

Each morning, we also choose what kind of person we are going to be that day. How are we going to show up in the world? How will we touch the hearts, minds, and souls of the people we come into contact with, regardless of how that looks: by phone, face to face, or even through our thoughts. Thoughts also "create" and can have a ripple effect on other people, Mother Earth, the solar system, and so on.

Because we get to choose everything, let's use the analogy in relationship to what we can create over an entire lifetime. I would highly recommend reading the inspiring and thought-provoking poem entitled, "The Dash" by Linda Ellis. The "dash" referenced in the poem, indicates the dash on our tombstone between our birth date and date of death. It represents how we have invested our time on this planet. Did we play life full out and touch the lives of others in a positive manner? Or, did we die with our dance still in us? Isn't real life about how we show up in the world? How we show up is a choice we make, whether to give or take, or have a balance of both. I call a good balance of both an "energy exchange."

We are all BEings of light in a physical body. What we experience, and how we touch the lives of other people, is determined to a large extent by what we decide to wear that day, that is, on a spiritual level. Remember, "We are spiritual beings having a human experience." Nothing happens TO us. It happens THROUGH us because we CHOOSE it. Therefore, we decide what we are going to experience every single day because we CREATE it.

On a deeper level everyone already knows that they are BEings of light and that light is energy. They have momentarily forgotten. Throughout this book, you will find many references to the fact that everything is energy. Energy shows up in many different ways. The frequency of its vibration determines whether or not the human eye can see it. We can often feel this energy through the many gifts we were given: our physical body, our soul, electromagnetic field, and through our emotional body, that is, IF we pay attention and raise our awareness.

Many people describe this light energy as the soul. Those who have had near death experiences have said that they saw a beautiful, bright, and pure white light. They experienced such a sense of love that it could not be described in human words and they are quite adamant about what they saw and felt. If we could describe in human words what we see as we are born, would we describe it in the same way?

Our physical lifetime, as we know it today, is limited by time and space. However, on a soul level, the measure of a lifetime could be like a day for us since the spirit or world of the soul is not limited by time and space. Everything is happening at once, and everything is infinite. This is difficult for the human mind to understand since our mind naturally wants to compartmentalize things into neat, tight boxes and patterns to establish an order that makes us feel comfortable and in control.

When we pay attention to our physical appearance rather than how we feel, we are saying to others and ourselves, "How I look to the outside world is more important to me than how I feel about myself." This is short-changing us, as well as others. We put a limit on our potential to see and experience more, instead of basing it on our own inner guidance system. When we allow that to happen, we will experience a significantly different lifestyle than what we intended when we came into this physical world.

Every choice is made for a reason, and so things happen for a reason. There are infinite choices that we could make. For example, tomorrow when you wake up you could either go for a leisurely walk around the neighborhood or a moderately strenuous hike through the forest. Somewhere in the ethers of a multi-dimensional universe that is infinite (and in a different reality), you chose to take the hike instead of the walk.

This may be difficult to initially wrap the mind around, but if we can keep an open mind and heart, it will give us a sense of peace, abundance, and clarity like never before. There will no longer be fear of that which we don't understand that has been causing us to feel anxiety, anger, regret, powerlessness, depression, or helplessness.

The things that we choose are the things that we are supposed to choose. There is no wrong decision. There is only "right. We choose it for a reason, based on the best information we have at the time. The choices we make either serve us, do not serve us, or perhaps a different choice could serve us in a better way.

It may be surprising, but God and the universe do not care what we choose. Each choice is simply a stepping-stone to the next. Even choices that do not serve us will eventually reveal to us in some way that making another choice (sooner or later) may be in our best interest. The key is paying attention to the results created by the choices we make. Are they serving our highest self or the best version we could create of ourselves? How will our choices affect others?

Think back to when you were a small child playing. On this day, you chose to play with blocks, instead of a spinning top. Your parents didn't care which toy you chose to play with. However, they did care about how you felt when you were playing. They wanted you to feel happy, content, secure, and loved, although they couldn't force you to be happy. All they could do was to place mechanisms or tools to happiness in your path. It was up to you to choose happiness.

It is the same scenario with the universe and God. There is no wrong. You are the one making choices that you label wrong, or perhaps you have been told by others that what you do or say is wrong. Furthermore, when groups of people get together to agree that something or someone is wrong, they spread the condition that I call the "you-are-wrong virus."

Which type of virus are you spreading? Is it the type of virus that makes people feel good and reminds them of their own God-given power, or is it the type of virus that cloaks their own energy from them?

As a brief side note, I want to shine a light on what may be going through the minds of some readers. If you are thinking, "If nothing is wrong, then I can do anything I want." This is true, however, if what you do is not out of love for the greater good of all, you will eventually create the opposite result than what you expected. More on this topic is discussed throughout this book.

When we get beyond the idea that something is wrong, we can live a very grounded and Divine life with a stable foundation. It doesn't matter what others think about the life you live. What does matter is how YOU feel. They cannot know you or your intent. They do not live in your body, heart, and mind. Other people's opinions of what we should be, do, have, look like, or feel like, can be good feedback to sift and sort through. However, it is important to keep in mind that advice from others is based on their own perspective of life. It is truly a reflection or mirror of how they live their life at that moment in time. That's not to say we cannot learn from others. It is important to note here again that all of us learn and teach others at the same time. Someone's level of education, title or measurement of success does not mean that they cannot learn from every person they meet if they are aware of this fact.

We do not have to own their reality and make it our own truth. It is necessary to listen to our own heart, pay attention to our emotions, and choose to live in joy. It is impossible to live in joy and also make something or someone else wrong. Opposites cannot occupy the same space at the same time.

Light is the purest form of energy. Light is also Love. Know this: You are a BEing of light. You are a light body. You are a body of light in a specific vibrational form. It is the same message in all of these sentences, but stated a bit differently each time. We are bodies of light, because we are energy. It could also be referred to as a body of energy, an energy body, or a BEing of energy. Which one most strongly resonates with you?

Anything that we can physically touch is simply a tool to help us experience what we choose to experience. We are not our body, our mind, or our emotions. They are all tools.

Although we may refer to our body as a physical biological organism, it is also something that we wear just like the clothing we cover it with to protect our biological organism from wear and tear, or the harmful rays of the sun. Our physical body helps us move around. It helps us to be mobile in order to experience what is called "the physical." Without it, we might in some form be able to do things, but we wouldn't have the sensations, or know how it feels to walk, feed ourselves, or dream for example.

Does it not free us up to know that everything we choose is RIGHT for us in one way or another at that moment in time? Every choice is connected to and affects everything else, which affects us as individuals in the cycle of life.

Previously I said that you were Light and Love. It may seem like these are two separate things, but they are not. It is all one, all connected, all encompassing and inclusive, because everything is energy.

Given this information (which by the way, we already know on a deeper level), who wouldn't make a choice from the space of love in every given moment? Imagine a world where everyone chose love. Higher evolved species already live in a cooperative environment that serves all, with no one or no-thing left out.

When the children of the blue planet called Earth (all of us collectively), raise their awareness to a level of heart coherence, cooperation and love, what we create will move beyond anything we've ever seen, even with our limited modern technology available today. What an amazing gift of love, called "choice." Only our Creator could have devised such a Divine matrix that was perfectly planned to experience itself over and over again in many different forms and dimensions.

Energy Exchange

As I've stated before and will continue to throughout this book, everything is energy; things that we can see and cannot see. There are also other dimensions that we cannot see because of our limited perspective and biological limitations here on this earth plane. Furthermore, there is an infinite number of everything.

This truth has been talked about and debated by some of the world's top spiritual and religious leaders for thousands of years. They have expressed and articulated it in their own words for their particular time period. They are different words, but the same message.

We are the ones who get to choose how we show up in the world in this lifetime. Do we shine our light fully? Shine it partially or cautiously? Do we let it shine upon everyone? Do we have a good balance of both giving and receiving? Are we taking from others, the planet, or it's resources? How much of our lifetime do we invest in giving? Will we give back to nature, to others, or to ourselves? I call this an "energy exchange." Balance is important in every area of our life. This can sometimes be a challenge, because many of us have caught the "busy bee syndrome" and have allowed it to control our lives through re-active responses. The fact is, we function better when we feel balanced even if it is for a few fleeting moments. It is in this space of near balance that we are at our best to help others. This is because everyone can be affected by everyone else's energy, unless they are grounded in their own authenticity. When we live in and honor our own authenticity, it acts as a protective layer or shield.

Since our emotions are our best indication of how we feel, I am always reminded to pay attention to how I feel from my "center point." (A center point is the energy place of balance within the body, which is located in the solar plexus area or chakra.) When we are crystal clear about how we want to feel, or in other words, the feelings that we want to intentionally create, that process intentionally creates our experience of reality. The difference between what you are feeling and how you want to feel is the window or door of opportunity to deeply KNOWING your truth.

The question is: Are you willing to go there and explore, or will you deny that you have and have had the power all the time to intentionally change your emotions? The longer you practice intentionally creating your emotions, the easier it becomes to distance yourself from the opposite feeling. This could involve undesirable situations, people, environments, or activities that do not line up with who you really are, or the emotion you want to create.

Over time that which you are not is immediately recognizable. Many people have done this so well, that they appear to be different than the flock of sheep that follow the mainstream mindset.

In the event that you have felt that you were socially inept or socially unintelligent, or perhaps that there was something wrong with you, I can assure you that is not true. If it does not feel good in your solar plexus, or does not create the emotion you want to intentionally create, respectfully back away from it. It is not in your best interest at that time. Remember to use HOW you feel as the measure. Just because it is not in alignment at that time, does not mean it never will BE. Everything happens in Divine right order. (Perhaps you know someone whom you judged to be socially inept, or socially unintelligent. Again, I can assure you that they are not. Let's look at this from another perspective while we step away from the place of EGO momentarily and with respect.)

While mainstream refers to people who are perceived to be different as odd, quirky, or anti-social, I see them as "Sensitives." This does not necessarily refer to someone who cries easily. A better way to describe it is that they are highly sensitive to the true intention of others in that moment. This may be from other people, situations, or circumstances. They can .feel" the energy to such a high degree, that they cannot ignore it, nor deny it. It is not unusual for them to immediately know when someone says or does something that is not in harmony with what they KNOW is really going on. Naturally, this would make anyone withdraw, since we are all giving off electromagnet energy that either attracts or repels. "Sensitives" (also known as "Empaths") can feel the repelling energy regardless of what is being said or done.

On some level, those who have the repelling energy know that the Sensitives are aware. The Sensitives often do not share what they know. This is not because they doubt themselves, but because they don't want to expend their valuable energy attempting to convince someone who would prefer to make them wrong, rather than make an effort to co-operate, honor and respect each other. Remember, many Sensitives understand energy and when they become aware of and live in this knowledge, they are acutely aware of how, when, and why they use their energy. Arguing or defending their position does not even occur to them. To them it would be as senseless as arguing over the correct color of their eyes.

Unfortunately, there are some people who, when they do not understand something, will attempt to belittle, either directly or subtly. They will sometimes resort to humiliation, intimidation, discrediting, or manipulating others to get them to agree with them. In this way, they feel more confident about what they believe, which is the only way they know to "get more power." They do not yet know that there is an unlimited amount of everything, including power, to go around.

There is some truth in the phrase, "strength in numbers," especially when it involves the process of creation and raising energy frequency. However, someone who is truly grounded and living their truth can stand alone in it. Throughout history, many people have been brutally beaten down physically and emotionally for having the confidence and courage to stand by their truth. I don't have to list them here, but opening your copy of the Bible would be a great start.

Sensitives know on an intuitive level (whether they are aware of it or not), when the energy isn't congruent with their path. Their heart and intuition tells them to back away. The media and our society as a whole, would have you believe that there is a specific way to be, and not be, socially. It can become so extreme, that some Sensitives begin to feel that there is something wrong with them. That is, until they realize that it is their heart that is leading them to live their truth, and their truth will not match that of anyone else.

Some Sensitives resist or deny the opposing energy and do not follow their truth because they fear rejection. They will usually develop many physical and mental health problems such as: depression, anxiety, weight gain, weight loss, joint issues, diabetes, heart dis-ease, and many more. They will suffer until they learn that they can 'In Deed' exist in a world where much of society denies the understanding of who we really are. When they learn that they are here to BE the catalyst that will open the windows of denial, their life path becomes clearer.

From my experience working with, talking to, and being around Sensitives, deep down they know what they must do, but temporarily have lost the courage to move forward.

Allow me to be clear about defining "repelling energy" in an honorable, respectful way. This type of energy is not "wrong," just different. Take for example, the positive and negative poles of the earth. They are not good or bad. They simply do not match up at the exact time and space. In fact they are so opposite that they will repel immediately, just like opposite ends of a magnet.

Would it surprise you to know that we are all born a Sensitive? Some of us stayed connected to that gift. Others followed people in power who seemed to have it all together, attempted to become like them, and so they lost their own way. The great news is that at any time, you can choose to use your power and recreate yourself anew, which in turn, will change your reality.

You have the power. You have always had it. It cannot be taken nor given away. You can only choose not to use it. Your choices will create your reality at any point in time.

You may have guessed by now that the reason I know about Sensitives is because I have been fully aware of this gift within me. I had my moments of denial as well. I tried many times to just fit in and "do life everyone else's way. Which by the way, wasn't working out for them either but they still labeled it as the "right" way to live.

I pretended so that those who knew that I knew (whom I mistakenly perceived to be more powerful) wouldn't target me. I dug a hole and buried it, by renaming it "my imagination". How about you? Now that you know everyone is born with it, how can you unearth your own power and use it for yourself and the greater good?

❤ ❤ ❤

3

DIVINE CONFIDENCE

It would be accurate to say that confidence comes from being comfortable with one's self. This means not only in private or with a few people, but also with everyone at all times. True confidence is about BEing your authentic self even when that means stepping away from others and who they want you to be. Following the crowd is often costly to your own morals or ethics. This does not suggest being difficult to get along with or being overly radical, unless of course, that is who you are.

I am suggesting, however, that as an evolving society, we would evolve much quicker if we were each authentic. BEing authentic means that we speak and live our truth not only with respect, but also with certainty. Imagine a world where everyone was authentic and stood in their truth with confidence. There would be no mind games and no reason to have competitive debates. We'd always know precisely where we stood in the world with ourselves and with other people. This would easily empower us to clear out the distracting clutter and focus on what is most important in every given moment. We would then create exactly what we want, instead of spending energy attempting to determine who is, or is not coming from a place of Divine Intention for only the greatest good of all.

Here are some questions to ponder, and it is important to be completely honest with one's self:

- Are you living your life or someone else's life?
- Are you creating your life around what matters most to you?
- Are you not sure, or do you think you are an exception to this question?
- Do you think that it doesn't apply to you because you are _____ or have _____? (Fill in the blanks.)

May I respectfully suggest the following exercise each and every time you don't feel in a state of joy, peace, and authenticity? Write out your responses so that you will be able to follow your progress.

Imagine that tomorrow when you awoke, your body was energized and in good health, and that you had all the money that you could possibly want. All you had to concern yourself with was how you would fully live the day and the days ahead. What would you do?

What would your day look like? If there was nothing to diffuse your attention away from designing your life around what mattered most, then what? Most people cannot answer this question. They have no idea what they might do.

Those that do answer it with conviction often have a generic, short answer. They might say, "I'd travel," or "I'd go shopping," or "I'd give to the poor," or "I'd lay around the house all day." Then what?

Unfortunately, society has made dreaming wrong and working 12 hours or more a day right. Mainstream society generally focuses on what's wrong with the world and expends little to no time or energy encouraging people to be their best, however that looks to them. Sometimes when they do encourage it, if it doesn't match their idea of what it should look like, they seek to make it wrong. Worse yet, a few will seek to publicly humiliate others.

Attempting to make someone else wrong is not about the other person at all. In fact, it is declaring to the world what you think is wrong with you. Many spiritual teachers have said that other people are our mirrors. What we see in them is what we like or dislike in ourselves. What we see in other people has little to do with them. In fact, their reality and perspective is often completely different than our own.

Have you ever been in a place of joy and you encounter someone who is in the opposite mindset as you? You may have a few pleasant words with them.

Suddenly, they spew a train of words that come so fast and furiously at you, that it leaves you stunned and wondering where that came from. How could they possibly have interpreted that in what you just said or did? That was not what you were currently experiencing or meaning at all.

I can assure you, it wasn't about you. They thought they saw something in you that triggered something about them that they didn't like. Instead of coming from a place of spiritual intelligence, thereby taking response-ability for their personal thoughts and actions, YOU happened to be the best target at that time. That is why what someone thinks of you is none of your business, because it has nothing to do with you. It reflects their own personal and private thoughts about themselves that they are projecting onto you.

Think about this for a moment. If you never knew and experienced the color purple, you would never recognize it, right? It is the same with kindness; if you had never experienced kindness you would never recognize it when someone was kind to you.

On the flip side, if you think everyone has underlying intentions or is out to overpower you, it isn't about them. That is the lens by which you view the world. That is the reality you created for yourself. It has little or perhaps nothing to do with what is actually happening. You are literally making it all up by the meanings you apply to it. We all are!

In any given situation with a thousand people present, all one thousand will see something different. What they experience will be based on what they have experienced in the past, as well as how they choose to perceive it. There may be similarities, but all will have recognized something slightly different. Therefore, you cannot recognize in others what you do not already know or have experienced.

Now that you've read the last few paragraphs, you have a choice. You can either disregard it, thinking that this is New Age nonsense and it couldn't possibly apply to you, or take the time to carefully consider how you are showing up to the world. People who are evolving toward spiritual intelligence already know that people wear their utmost secrets about how they feel about themselves on their sleeves. Their intention is evident, and clearly indicates why they treat others as they do.

What does intention mean? We all know people who are kind and help others. Perhaps that describes you too. Why are they kind, and why do they help others? How do they benefit? Is it coming from EGO (Edging God Out) or pure Divine Intention for the greater good of everyone? I like that acronym because it makes us think on a deeper level, about the true intentions behind any action that we take. God would always choose to act with Divine Intentions for the greater good of all.

From my experience, as a person who has manifested (created) many things in my life, I can tell

27

you that what you create is all about your intention. When your intention in helping others is mostly from the EGO needs of fame, fortune, and/or applause, and not for the greater good of all, manifesting what you want will not work long term. It may show up, but will be temporary; and it is highly possible too, that you may not want what you created! Divine Intention is about caring enough to not enable people, but to empower them. This reveals to them that they already have the power to take action without dependency on anything outside of themselves. As soon as you make someone dependent on you, you distract them from their spiritual intelligence and create the illusion of pumping up your EGO. You are making it all about you and the power you perceive to have over them. As you will later learn, you cannot take someone's power. It is an illusion.

It may shock you to learn that the information you are reading here (or have ever learned), you already know. You've simply forgotten that you know. All the information that ever was is still floating around in the ethers, including thoughts and ideas. For this reason, there is nothing new, and since there is no time or space, no past, present or future, it is all happening at once.

You are able to assess this knowledge at any given time by getting into a space of true Divine Intention, prayer, meditation, appreciation, or however you choose to connect with it. Once we make the decision to move forward, we have the option to grab hold of the ideas and concepts that will move us forward or not. That is often why when someone else comes up with an idea we relate to, we realize we already thought of it or knew it. The difference is, one person decided to move forward with the thought they grabbed, and the other ignored it, thinking it was a "dreamers" idea. Which would you rather choose to do? Thoughts are there for a reason; act upon those that serve us. Thoughts that lack Divine Intention and do not serve are there to give us an opportunity to choose differently so we can feel our way to becoming closer to our authentic self.

Accept & Share Your Greatness

We are all born with abilities and gifts. Personally, I refer to these gifts, as our greatness. No one was left out of the greatness line when the gifts were handed out. In the trauma, drama, and manipulation of our lives, we have forgotten that we have gifts, or we bury them because we are afraid to use them. Many times we fear that if we allow others to see our gifts, they will feel threatened or may not understand.

When we forget or choose to ignore our gifts, we tend to focus more on the weaknesses in ourselves, and therefore we more often see the weaknesses in other people. Although we are constantly attempting to improve ourselves, we are looking at what we don't want or would like to eliminate from our lives, instead of what we DO want to create and bring into our lives for the experience called "joy."

This is not new. Books that are centuries old, including the Bible, contain the same message, but somehow, most of humanity has forgotten it, or again, have chosen to ignore it for their own purposes. It is really all about what you want and are open to seeing. Judgment only serves our EGO. BEing open to seeing without judgment is the main characteristic of all visionaries.

We are all born unique. Twins have similar attributes, but they are still different. We are each an individualized fingerprint and partial DNA of the Divine. All animals and plants are also each unique. Zebras illustrate this perfectly, as their markings are giant fingerprints, and no two zebras' markings are alike. No two snowflakes ever fallen have been identical at a microscopic level, nor will they ever be. Why then, do we not see that we each bring some type of greatness (or gift) to humankind? When shared, these talents or gifts are meant to help others along their path. Since we are all unique, our paths and how we choose to live our lives must also be unique; yet we still end up at the same destination.

Meanwhile, the majority of our species seems to think, or wants to make it wrong, that people are on different paths. They want everyone to be just like they are, think the way they do, and agree with them, or there may be some kind of consequence. Why do you think that is? We encounter it every day, don't we?

Could it be that they lack Divine Confidence in BEing who they really are? Are they afraid of walking their path alone and just as importantly, are they willing to accept their own greatness? Could it be that in order to feel good about themselves, they feel they must surround themselves with people who agree with them?

Sometime ago, I was involved with a leadership workshop experience where we were told to wear a button for nine weeks no matter where we were, and what we were doing. The button boldly stated, "Accept Your Greatness." I was also to spontaneously tell everyone I encountered, the greatness that I saw in him or her.

Can you imagine my reaction and the reactions of the other 110 people in our workshop? For me personally, many thoughts started racing through my mind about where I would be during those nine weeks and whom I would be with. What would they think? In my mind, I started making excuses about why I couldn't wear it 100% of the time. At that moment, something that a world-renowned leadership author once told me came to mind, "How you do anything is how you do everything." After being given a challenge that I chose to accept, I then found myself making excuses and talking myself out of the 100% commitment. Where else did that show up in my life?

I suppose I could have made the choice not to make the commitment at all. But then if I had, where else did that show up? Furthermore, that would have hindered me in making an amazing quantum leap of personal and spiritual growth. I'm so glad I didn't make that choice. It would not have served me.

The awkwardness didn't last long. The rewards of wearing the button far surpassed the initial uncomfortable feeling. It became a welcomed accessory that I wore during everyday activities including shopping, doing errands, exercising, having dinner out with family and friends, during corporate meetings and spiritual conferences. I wore it everywhere.

Would you be interested in hearing about what happened? I thought so:

Part 1: When most people noticed my Greatness Button their eyes lit up, especially when I told them the greatness I saw in them. Too many people today are not acknowledged for their strengths. They tend to dwell in the past or future, instead of celebrating who they are right now. A few people thought it was okay for me, but not for them - after all they had it all together. They didn't feel they needed to change, and personal development was for the weak or emotionally unstable. Interesting thought process, but I had no judgment. A few people turned it around on me, and told me the greatness they saw in me, which I accepted with grace.

The objective of the exercise was not only to raise awareness in us individually, but also in others so they could step up to their greatness. For me, it meant accepting the various reactions, both positive and negative, without judgment; just letting people make of it what they wanted at that moment in time. You see, giving to others is a great gift, but BEing willing to receive is part of the gift that we give ourselves. Rejecting a gift from someone is not honoring the part of that person that wants to give; nor is it honoring the part of you that wants to receive.

Would you like to accept the challenge of wearing this button for nine weeks to see what you can learn about yourself and others? It takes focus, commitment, and courage. I know you have all three, because you were born with them.

To get your own Greatness Button while supplies last, go to: www.ShareYourGreatness.com.

The Challenge

Wear this button with pride for nine weeks every day all day, regardless of where you go, or whom you are with. It is a good thing if you are uncomfortable wearing it. You will take it off only to shower and sleep. As soon as you receive it in the mail, put it on right away. Be open to telling everyone that acknowledges seeing it (and those that you know intuitively, need to hear it the most), what greatness you see in him or her.

Some people choose to ignore the button. Where else does that show up in their life? What other gifts do they choose not to receive? What other incredible experiences and opportunities are they ignoring?

Watch others' reactions without judgment. This is an amazing exercise to practice reducing the judgments that are not serving anyone. Pay attention to what you notice about their reactions, and about your thoughts and feelings in response to their reaction. Notice what you observe without judging yourself, because this exercise will help you as well as the other person. We are students and teachers at the same time - all the time.

So what do you say to them? Simply say the first thing that comes into your heart without running it through your head for approval or assurance that it doesn't sound silly, or that it sounds cool and is inspiring. For example, I might say, "Sally, the greatness I see in you is your servant heart," or "John, the greatness I see in you is your perseverance."

In order for you to totally appreciate this self-discovery journey, you'll want to experience wearing the button yourself for nine weeks, if you dare. Even if you think you know what will happen, I can assure you that you will be surprised. If you think this exercise will not have value or teach you anything, what is that telling you about yourself? No judgment here. Only you will know.

So as not to influence your experience by telling you of mine and the entirety of what I learned about myself, and others, I won't publicize my entire experience with the use of the button here.

After wearing my button for nine weeks, our leadership workshop group convened, and we were taken into the downtown streets of a large metropolitan area. There, we were to approach total strangers on the street and "sell" the button.

Most of us did not want to. We had all grown very attached to the deep relationship connections it had brought to us. In addition, many questions came to mind: How much would we sell it for? Why would anyone want to buy the button? What would people think? What was even the point? Well, find out in Part 2 of the Greatness Button Story. After you've worn your button for nine weeks, I'll email you Part 2. You've guessed it. There is a Part 3.

Go ahead. Step into your greatness today. Own your greatness and then SHARE it with others at: www.shareyourgreatness.com

Now imagine a world where everyone sincerely notices the greatness (gifts) in others. Could that even be possible? Yes. It would involve a shift of enough people choosing love, compassion, peace and kindness over greed, power, ego, competitiveness, and being right, instead of BEing happy. Not only could it BE possible, but it would also change the world. It doesn't take that many people to create a paradigm shift in consciousness. It is a simple choice. The problem exists because people are afraid of what might happen if they choose not to play the game, to lead instead of follow, and BE who they really are.

The other element missing in this life for many people is that we do not personally acknowledge people for their greatness. In other words, tell them what we notice. We may copy them, and subtly try to be like them, and sometimes we might even take their ideas; but we rarely make an effort to give people credit where credit is due. This is not about stroking someone's ego so that they like us. It is simply acknowledging them for their valuable part in our own evolution and thanking them for BEing a significant part of it.

Every single person in this universe is connected whether we accept it or not. We are all small twigs of the greater whole of the same tree. Co-operation (co-creation) instead of competition is always a choice. The outcome over a period of time will reveal the true intention behind any experience. It is transparent for all to see in the results that are created.

Intention is not about putting it out there in the universe, and by some magic, it shows up. Hoping will not draw it to you. All hoping will do is draw more hoping to you. It is about placing it in your heart with the intention that everyone will win, and then taking the necessary and deliberate steps without forcing. When you force anything, it will resist every time, making it a struggle. It may seem like it is working on the surface, but the results will always be temporary. A good way to determine if you are forcing any situation is by how difficult the process feels.

The person who is resisting is not in a good place in that particular space and time. If you say it to them and it is their truth, that is good. If they see it, say it, live it and it is their truth, that is the strongest truth of all. Remember too, that your path to truth is yours and unique to you. Theirs may be completely different.

When someone is willing to do or say anything to get whatever he or she thinks will make them look better in the eyes of others, unhealthy competition meets unhealthy intention. On a long-term basis, this will create the exact opposite of what is wanted. It is so much simpler, and creates less drama, to just take action from the heart. Drama creates trauma to everyone involved.

The interesting thing is that we are all born knowing our truth. We forget it, ignore it, permit others to manipulate it, but not because we are afraid of failure. We are afraid of success. We intuitively know how powerful we are as "co-creators." We avoid stepping into it, because after all, we would have to keep up with ourselves. Meanwhile, we set up obstacles called resistance and distractions, as a veil to hide from ourselves. As we know, veils are semi-transparent. We can still see through them. Therefore, our higher self (our spirit) continues to call to us to step into our truth, which when acted upon will lead us eventually to our core purpose (our highest purpose).

The Intimacy Escape

As we recognize and acknowledge the greatness in others, be aware of how sarcasm and teasing will create the opposite result. What I mean by that is we often mistake joking around with sarcastic remarks and teasing as a mechanism to show how much we like or love someone. These techniques are a wedge between that person and you becoming truly intimate with them on a deeper level. Joking and sarcastic remarks are an avoidance of intimacy. I'm not talking about intimacy on a sexual level unless that is the relationship you have with a particular person. I am talking about using jokes at another's expense and often referring to it as "just kidding," "all in fun," or "having a sense of humor," to show how much we like someone (or send a mixed message.) This form of illusionary intimacy creates division and confusion for the other person while it builds a much bigger and stronger wall around your own heart. It's a false sense of protection and a false sense of intimacy. Being open, honest and uplifting to people is the path to deeper intimacy.

Understand that I am not saying that a sense of humor is bad. Quite the contrary because laughing and BEing sincerely jovial is the quickest way to BEing in the moment and experiencing a glimpse of eternity. A sense of humor though is often used as a buffer between people BEing real with other people, putting all cards on the table face up. If you are using humor as an intimacy protection device, stop. You cannot love yourself or all others fully with a protective wall around your heart.

I Am and You Are

Who are you? Why are you here? What is your purpose? Have you done any soul searching lately and/or looked deep into your heart? I'm sure you've asked and answered these questions of yourself at least once in your lifetime. Let's examine it from the "I AM" perspective:

As previously stated, I AM a spiritual BEing having a human experience. This may be a bit difficult to wrap the mind around, but bear with me a moment. First, let me briefly focus on telling you what I am NOT. Even though focusing on anything I am not does not serve me, it is being used here only to help the reader experience the contrast between the two statements.

I am not my mind; I am not my body; I am not my emotion. I am not what I do for a living. I am not someone's property. I am not any of these things. I get to choose how I finish this sentence, in every breath I take every second of every day: I AM _____.

When I do this, I create my reality the very moment I say or think it. It is said that the mind is not capable of understanding the word NOT. The message that the mind gets is, "I am my mind. I am my body. I am ___." Now that we know this truth, "I am" statements that do not serve us can easily be flipped. In this way, the statements look at who you really are instead of who you are not. Which leads to what you WANT to create instead of what you don't want in your life.

Abraham-Hicks have an amazing exercise I learned years ago called "The Focus Wheel." I highly recommend using this tool to help you begin intentionally recreating what you are thinking about and move your thoughts into forward thinking, creative statements that serve you and others.

❤ ❤ ❤

4

YOUR EMOTIONS ALWAYS HAVE
& ALWAYS WILL MATTER

There is a tendency, particularly in today's society, to think that what we feel or sense does not matter, that only what we do or how we act counts. Allow me to explain why it serves us best to create a balance of both.

Whenever we do anything that is not of the best and highest intention for all involved, it may be difficult, if not impossible to manifest (create). It is necessary to align our heart and our head for the greater good of self, and everyone else, before doing whatever it is we plan to do. The process will then fall into place smoothly, with all cooperative components arriving exactly when and where they are needed. It will be fun and everyone will say, "Let's do it again!"

In contrast, when forcing an issue, even if we were to somehow manage to create the results we want, it would be short-lived. When we come from an intention of win-lose or win-kill, it all backfires by creating something no one will want. It is human nature to then become resistant to attempting it again, because it was such a struggle that opened a big bag of crazy ugly, so to speak. No one wants or needs more drama. Drama equals trauma.

You have a natural ability to intuitively know when energy that is coming toward you doesn't feel good. You will feel it in your heart – not your head. Let your heart be your guide. If it makes you feel bad, it is then your obligation to honor yourself, and move away from that low-frequency energy. That does not mean that the situation or the people involved are necessarily bad or wrong. It simply means the energy coming toward you is not a match at this time, and that you are definitely feeling it. You are not imagining it; start trusting yourself.

It is important to note that certain emotions will surface from time to time and that they are built into our DNA. These types of emotions will trigger in us, what is commonly known as, a fight or flight reaction. They save our life when we are in serious danger.

The low-frequency energy that I mentioned is not the same as the fight or flight reaction, although it is often thought to be and confused with the same. The emotion I am speaking of is called "emotional confusion."

This often occurs when something happened to us, or we have done something to someone else in the past, and this data is pulled from our mind's memory banks. Therefore, we assume that because we re-act that way, everyone else does. We think everyone lives in that reality; they do not. This is an example of applying our meaning to events that create a reality that doesn't serve anyone.

How do we distinguish between the feeling of the emotionally charged energy that creates "emotional confusion" coming from past data and our own Divine Intuition? Emotional Confusion causes us to want to flee or fight. Divine Intuition energy is not charged by emotion. It is felt and has no sense of urgency to lash out and save ones EGO.

When we don't feel good about ourselves, a situation, are ignored, or are in a position where we cannot openly speak our own truth without judgment, we do not feel heard. This never makes us feel good unless we know how to intentionally make ourselves feel better. When people do not feel good about themselves they are not producing to their maximum capability, which affects everyone in some way.

Our emotions are always an indicator of what is going on in our life at the very moment we are feeling and experiencing it. This is true, whether we are on the right track moving forward, or moving away from what we want. Our emotions are one of the greatest gifts we were given. They are there for a reason and not to be ignored. Why would we want to ignore one of our greatest gifts?

The challenge is to determine if it is Emotional Confusion based on a past experience that was traumatic. Is it an experience that your mind has pulled out of its memory/data banks for comparison purposes? Or is it something you need to pay closer attention to because it is your inner radar system (Divine Intuition) detecting an external energy frequency that does not serve you? Whatever it is, your job is to help yourself feel better. We have an obligation to care for ourselves with honor and respect. Nothing is more important to you than how you feel at all times. This statement is so important, that it bears repeating multiple times.

The Law of Knowing

Your life may be good now, but what would happen if you changed one single belief and/or your perspective? Flipping that switch could change the way the world is working for you right now in a better way and in turn, affect the lives of many other people. What if everyone in the world did that for just five minutes? You could never, nor would you want to go back. Once you know something, you cannot un-know it. It is law. I call it the Law of Knowing: www.lawofknowing.com.

Trying to un-know something you know will pull you apart, because it is like having one foot in one reality and one in another. This causes depression, anxiety, manipulative behaviors, desperation, intimidation, and anger, not to mention physical ailments - all caused by what is perceived as stuck energy. What a simple explanation for feeling stuck. Would you agree? If you feel stuck, it is because you are choosing to live in that reality! Pay close attention to how you feel. Your emotions are an indicator as to what is going on in your life. You cannot move forward when you are looking backward and re-acting to the past.

Re-acting to the past is like watching an actor, re-enact the same scene of the same play over and over again. The audience becomes annoyed and frustrated while the actor and audience become bored. What do most people do when they become bored? They do things that do not serve their highest self. Boredom is merely a symptom of not taking forward action. Forward action is the process of creation.

At a deeper heart and soul level, people know that looking backward is holding them in an illusion of a trapped state, but their mind is still saying something different. That "something" is that their spirit/soul is calling to them to change. This could be the change of a career or relationship, letting go of something they are resisting, attitude, nutrition, exercise, daily activities, different friends, location, spending more time with their children, etc. or a combination of several of these. There is an innate sense of knowing that it is the right direction in which to move. What is currently happening in their life is not working, and although it may have served them at one time, it no longer does. In this case, they have grown into a higher awareness of who they are, and can no longer deny it. Have you ever heard the saying, "Don't die with your dance still in you?"

What often happens is that people become confused, anxious, increasingly depressed, angrier, and more fearful. It is usually at that point that they start to take or increase medications. Meanwhile, the medications mask the real problem. The problem is that they are trying to un-know something or ignore it, which causes the illusion of being stuck. Remember, energy is always in motion. The first indication of this happening is your emotions and how you feel. Emotions, left dishonored, create dis-ease and over time manifests into physical illnesses that continue to get worse when denied or ignored.

Eventually, it comes back like a haunting, until the person faces it directly and moves through it. In other words, all it takes is accepting what is already known, and then flipping the switch to change a belief system that is no longer working. This causes movement forward, which eventually picks up momentum until you have created what you desire. Unfortunately, the alternative is departing this physical planet with the dance still inside of you, which is what many people do.

This is a concept that is often difficult for the human mind to imagine. The more we get involved with what we don't know, the wider we open our heart to let go of EGO, and welcome in the life we were meant to live. We also find that there is far more that we don't know, than that we do know.

Remember that previously used metaphor. Simply flipping a switch and making it "okay" to shift a small part of our belief system, could change the world, as we now know it. Yes, YOU can affect the entire world by simply flipping that switch for five minutes. Don't allow naysayers to belittle you of the power that you know you have and were born with. You have the right to use your power for the greater good of all, including yourself. Those who undermine you are choosing the illusion of being stuck in a place of limited thinking in their own world; they just don't know it yet. That's okay. We are where we are for a reason. However, convincing you to think in any way, other than your own unique self, distracts you from your power. It dis-honors you for BEing you. This is the only way they know to survive and what they believe gives them more power. Taking power from others is an illusion. There is a scarcity mentality that drives them and they usually don't mean to hurt you. They think it's the only way to feel better. There always has been and always will be enough power to go around.

The Gift of Choice

The great news is that we have been given another gift. If you haven't noticed yet, that gift is the gift of choice.

Choice is available to us anytime and it can be extremely empowering. The question is: When will we flip the switch? Will we do it right now, in weeks, or years from now? We each get to decide how long we stay in that illusionary stuck position. Choice is a wonderful gift that has been there inside of us all along. It was never outside of us, nor was it too complicated to understand. WE make it complicated. We also create the experiences of our lives by the choices we make. The speed in which we make the choices determines how fast we move through life on the magic carpet ride of joy, or how long we stay sitting on the magic carpet, imagining we are stuck in a place that doesn't serve us. We then often point our finger at others, as if they are the ones response-able for making our magic carpet move. It is our response-ability individually to make our own magic carpet spring into action.

In some multi-dimensional universe every choice is being played out. It is all happening at the same time: past, present, and future. There is no separateness of what we know as time. Remember, there is only an infinite loop of cycles in motion. Life is not linear; but circular. Everything is happening all at once. All we have to do is reach out and grab the choice → that creates the emotion → that creates the reality → that puts us in the place → that serves up the delicious meal of joy called "life."

Human Energy

Always pay attention to how you are feeling. Eventually, you learn to honor yourself, and walk away from any situation that is not in alignment with your truth. The more you practice BEing aware, the quicker you will feel it as it happens. How do you know? You will sense that something is not quite a match with you. Sometimes it will show up subtly; you know something is off but you cannot quite identify it. Other times, it is so powerful that it is in your face immediately. It takes practice but over time you will be amazed at how much you have been missing that was always there.

A side note on human energy: When referring to energy, it does not necessarily refer to someone who is energetic with enthusiasm, talks fast, or moves quickly. There are many reasons why someone would act in these manners; it often has little to do with a high-frequency vibration.

When you are consciously aware and practice noticing it, you can easily feel a low vibration when you walk into a room. You are feeling this with the frequency vibration of your own magnetic field. Of course, the exception would be if your vibration were very low at that time and matches external energy coming toward you. We are all radio frequency antennas picking up signals all the time. As long as you are physically in your current body you cannot shut it off. Even when you leave your physical body, your energy transfers into another form.

This is also NOT about social intelligence, reading body language, noticing micro-expressions, and the many manipulative power games people play. It is about the one thing that we are all able to do, and that is feel energy. Since we ARE energy, we are magnetically drawn to matching energy and are naturally repelled by polar opposites, just like two magnets. Again, this is not judgment on good or bad. One end of a magnet is not any better than the other; both are needed.

Have you noticed that when you are with someone who is not in the same space as you, that it does not feel good? This is because in that space and time your magnetic energies repel each other. It is perfectly okay to walk away politely, and in fact, that is what I'd suggest, in order to honor all of those present <u>with grace and respect</u>. Two or more repelling" energies that are near each other will affect an entire room of people and all animals that are present.

Watch the animals the next time you feel this low-vibrational energy. They are great antennas. In fact, animals, babies, and small children are far more connected to Source energy than adults, and are excellent at "BEing in the moment." Animals can teach us a lot about how life is meant to be lived. Nothing is more important to them at all times than feeling good. Why is it that we have a tendency to think we are smarter on many levels than they are? Adult humans allow themselves to be pulled away from "who they really are." Meanwhile, we choose to ignore, belittle, or eliminate things we don't understand and sometimes consider these re-actions as fun or entertainment. Babies, small children, and animals always live in their heart space of joy; always being who they know they really are.

Although we teach children, we are both teacher and student at the same time. Until we understand what that means, we will continue to struggle as a society. We will continue to ask the same questions that we've asked for thousands of years, as quoted by Neale Donald Walsch, "Who am I? Why am I here? Why isn't it working?"

Feel Your Way to Feeling Better

Emotions are a natural and necessary radar system built into our BEing. They make us aware in which direction we are moving on our own unique path of truth. Are we moving closer to our truth, or are we moving away from who we really are?

Many people give in to the illusion of being "stuck" and spend too much time trying to analyze their emotions. However, we get into serious trouble when we allow the opposite to be true. It only makes sense that there must be a balance. Never allow yourself to suppress or ignore your emotions, or let anyone else encourage you not to "feel" a certain way, or belittle you for having emotions. Your emotions are there for a reason; you were born with them. Emotions are your built-in, God-given gift to let you know the path you are on. They will either help you to create or hold you back by looking at something that does not deserve your attention or serve you. It's your choice how you use them or if you use them.

There is a process I call the pivotal point. We have all had many pivotal points in our lives. A pivotal point is the degree and speed in which you refocus your attention and change your thoughts, which creates a massive change and often quickly. This allows you to feel better even if it is in the slightest way. It is one step at a time, *unless it isn't*.

Imagine for a moment that you are in an environment in which you feel you have no control. Not a pleasant visualization, but bear with me for a moment. You cannot change what is going on around you, because it is not about you. Trying to will only put you deeper into an emotion that does not serve you.

The only thing that is about you and what you CAN control, is what is going on inside of you. With that said, as soon as you feel an emotion, notice it, and honor it. Honoring an emotion simply means you are not judging or beating yourself up for having it. Here are the affirmations to say to yourself with compassion and Divine Intention when you feel an unwanted emotion:

- I honor the fact that I am having this feeling. I do not know why. I do not know how it happened. It is no ones fault.

- I will intentionally cause myself to feel better, because I know I can only control what happens inside of me and not what is going on outside of me. What is outside of me is not about me.
- I am going to think a thought that brings me joy, even if it is the next best thought that brings the slightest better feeling.
- I will continue to do this until I reach a state of peace and joy.
- I will do this each time, immediately after I recognize an emotion or feeling that is not serving me, or is in opposition to who I am, so that I may move closer to my own unique truth.
- The more I practice this, the more I will become clearer about who I am and the quicker I will notice things that do not serve my truth and which are not in alignment with my own core values.

This is not about taking back your own power. Your power is always there and has been waiting for you at any time you want it. "Feel" your way toward it. Again, the importance of this statement bears repeating. Nothing is more important than "how" you feel, and living in your authentic truth. Depending on others to tell you how you should or shouldn't feel is like keeping your internal power switch in the off position.

Understand fully that giving your power away is an illusion and only serves to keep you in the misconception of stuck-ness. You have the power, always have and always will. No one can actually physically, emotionally, or spiritually take away your power. Nor can anyone actually gain more power by attempting (whether aware or unaware) to take someone else's power. That too is an illusion. That is easily demonstrated by their addictive need to continuously attempt to gain more power from others. The charge they feel is EGO. It is not anything close to high-frequency energy. It was not done with Divine Intention. Therefore, the feeling is temporary because it was an illusion from the beginning. It isn't an addiction to power as some reference it. It is an addiction to feeding the EGO with the illusion.

It is important that you do this exercise with Divine Intention from your heart for the greater good of everyone, without a single person left out. Whenever we experience a negative emotion toward someone, it is an indicator that we are moving in the opposite direction; we are not serving everyone's best interest.

You can do this exercise to the extreme of the continuum, and create a pivotal point for yourself quickly. You may also choose more subtle change. Sometimes we wait until something is about to happen, or has happened, to create a quick-change pivotal point. We continually ignore our own intuition and over time, it wears us down. Worse yet, we may have experience degrees of emotional or physical pain in order to wake up and create a change that has been calling us for a long time.

Unfortunately, some people are so uncomfortable living in their own skin that they choose to leave this physical body and return to spirit. When this occurs, they are cutting their life short and taking their Divine Grace from others who are their students and their teachers.

When you do not feel the emotion you want to feel, reach for a better feeling thought immediately. Once you start to feel better, you will be able to create even better thoughts, thus creating your experience.

As I mentioned earlier, what you experience is going to look and feel differently than what other people experience. It may be similar but never exact. This is because it is based on several factors:

- All experiences that have happened in the past.
- The memory data collected, past and present.
- The meanings we give to all of it.

It is the meaning and often the strength of the feeling that triggers a re-action, but it is our response that will determine the outcome. Others react differently than we do, because their perspective is different. We must recognize and honor that. No one is wrong. They are only viewing it from a different perspective. Remember that the meaning you give it creates the intensity of your reality, either moving you closer to your own truth or farther from it.

Have you ever insisted on making someone wrong? When we do this we are not honoring what they see as their truth, or the path that they have chosen in that moment in time. Of course, we have all done this a number of times. Since others are our mirrors, when we do this, we are moving farther away from our own truth. This is the exact opposite of what appears to be happening. People think that if they can prove others wrong, or force them to agree, that it makes them more right. When in truth, the "I WIN" emotion is an illusion that will not last long. It becomes a continual loop of self-disempowerment, because they will soon seek out others to make wrong in order to get that emotional high again. You do not have to make anyone wrong to feel good about yourself – ever.

In truth, the answer is inside of them. It is futile for them to look outside of themselves and try to force people to agree. Everything they've always wanted and will ever want already exists inside of them. Attempting to convince anyone of anything is not about the other person. They are attempting to convince themselves.

With that said, let's explore this in another way – a way that is commonly misunderstood.

If I know my eyes are brown in the light a human eye can see, why would I ever feel the need to convince others of it? How about you?

If I recognized, accepted, and share my greatness gifts with others, would I continually feel the need to compete with others so as to feel better about myself?

No, of course not. Attempting to convince anyone of anything is not about them; it is about convincing ourselves. When we live confidently on our path, what others do is not important. They are creating their own story. Their story is not about you, *unless it is*. Meaning -- unless they choose for it to BE.

The Truth About the Law of Attraction

The Law of Attraction states, "The essence of that which is like unto itself, is drawn." It only makes sense that if we want to create an intentional reality we must intentionally choose our thoughts. As we practice this, we draw to us situations, events, people, relationships, animals, objects, and experiences that match what it is we want or intend to create. This is because everything is energy and they match our energy frequency, *unless they don't*.

The same thing happens if we allow ourselves to go in the opposite direction. This takes us farther and farther down the endless, but circular spiral of drama and trauma, attracting to us more of the same. This is the true Law of Attraction.

Practicing the law of attraction isn't about hoping, wishful daydreaming, and having things magically appear. The true Law of Attraction is about raising our heart coherence - our electromagnetic frequency. This is where Divine Intention comes in for the greater good of all. Although we cannot control what another person thinks, feels, does or says, if our true intention is pure, we will draw to us the energy frequency of whatever it is we match. The very important exception to understand, and this is why I previously stated, *"unless they don't,"* is that we will draw the matching frequency to us until the "Law of Opposites" shows up. The Law of Opposites is a reminder system of who we really are, what we are doing here, and what we said we wanted to create. That is when we get a chance to strengthen BEing Spiritually Intelligent and create monumental personal and spiritual growth in ourselves. More on the Law of Opposites will be explored later in this book.

However, when what you said you wanted shows up, it may not appear exactly as you expected it to look. Be open and non-resistant to however it materializes. Remember it is often a bridge or stepping stone for something even better to manifest, and it will.

As a side note and because I want to clear up any potential for biased misinformation, the definition of manifest is, "to make clear or evident to the eye or the understanding; show plainly; to prove; put beyond doubt or question." We ALL "manifest" by our thoughts, words, and deeds. Some of us have just forgotten that we can, and do. The word is nothing to be feared. Use the word "create," if you prefer.

Another way to describe the process of manifestation is to envision the action and then create. Envisioning our desires and dreams are only one step. Dream boards are a powerful visualization tool to help us hold that space of our vision. However, envisioning ourselves working through the actions steps is the catalyst to put it into motion.

We give birth to new ideas, new relationships, and new experiences all of the time. We are a creation machine with infinite possibilities, infinite choices, and infinite resources.

When we expect something to look a certain way, we are trying to control and force things outside of us. It rarely shows up for the long term the way we expect. When we do that, we are closing the door of opportunity to see a bridge that will lead us to the very thing we wanted.

The "how" it shows up is not as important as the intention of it being a win-win for everyone. In this way, we are raising our vibration (frequency). I often refer to this as aligning our head with our heart. Another way to look at it is, that we are all walking and breathing biological radio antennas, pulsating energy waves out into the world. We are BEings of light energy.

What are you pulsating? The energy frequency we give off can affect other things around us to some degree. It can eventually affect the entire planet and everything both seen and unseen in the universe.

Animals can instinctively feel it. Some people feel it to varying degrees, but may not understand what they are feeling. Unfortunately, these people often become depressed or anxious because someone else has convinced them they are wrong even though in their heart, they know differently. There are also some who can see energy fields, called auras, around people, objects, and animals.

It is our personal response-ability to raise our own frequency. It is not someone else's job. What if we were all attentive to how we are showing up in the world? How different would all of our lives be if we all came from a place of Divine Intention, passion, compassion, and any other positive word you want to place after the word Divine?

We would all be pulsating at an amazing frequency that would raise this planet into a higher evolved place to live, grow, learn, and teach. This is what life is all about, and best of all, this Divine Intention can be accessed at any time we choose. The power is and has always been within us.

To recap, when we desire something strongly enough, in order to receive it, we must be sure that we are coming from a place of Divine Intention. Meaning that:

- Our desire is for the greater good of everyone, with no one intentionally left out.
- We allow by knowing we are never in control of the circumstances or anything that exists outside of ourselves.
- We allow by accepting and going with the flow; that is, not trying to force it with our own agenda.

- We are open to seeing it show up in many different ways and not expecting it to look a specific way.

For example: If you say you want to write a hit song and it does not happen in the timeframe you planned, I suggest that your emotions, mind, and heart are not lined up with Divine Intention for the benefit of all. However, if you are willing to open your heart and mind to all possibilities, you will eventually meet someone that will lead you to the person you are looking for. That could be a voice coach, a singer/songwriter, composer, someone in a band that can help you, or someone who has the same desires that you do. When you find someone with the same desire, together you can create something more powerful than you could individually.

Always keep your eyes, mind, and heart open. Everyone we meet arrives in our lives for a reason in Divine right timing. Humans often judge each other by appearance, thus ruling out the possibilities, just because someone has the "wrong" look. By doing this, we are limiting ourselves, and each other.

Because other people are our mirrors, it is a judgment about our self. We are not hurting them, only ourselves. Most of all, we are missing the point of that person arriving in our life at that moment in time.

Call it God, the Universe, Source, your Highest Self, whatever is most meaningful to you. All are correct. It is YOUR truth if what you believe and know moves you to a place of love for everything and everyone. Jesus never made anyone wrong. He taught acceptance of everyone regardless of what kind of "look" they had, including prostitutes, people with leprosy, the homeless, the wealthy, or any place in between. Jesus taught us to accept everyone for who they are and to respect their truth. This is often referred to as Christ Consciousness and a beautiful model to live by.

Therefore, stay open to what is happening because it may very well be the catalyst or bridge, to help you get what it is you really want. The reason that it may go in a different direction, instead of a direct line, is that there is something to be learned along the way. Perhaps it is to raise your awareness of what is happening so that you learn to stay in your heart space with Divine Intention.

When you stay in the place of heart coherence and you are vibrating at a high frequency, things will happen so fast one after another, after another. You will be so amazed at your power to create, that it may even scare you.

There have been countless times in my life when I have consciously put the brakes on or had one foot on the gas and one on the brake at the same time. Yes, you are right, that never works out well!

Actually, everything I wanted was showing up – boom, boom, boom. Perhaps not in the way I originally expected, but showing up, none-the-less. My greatest fear has always been speed. How would I ever keep up with myself?

I know for a fact that you have experienced this multiple times. Why? Because we are all natural born creators. Once we put passion behind the action, miracles occur – every time.

We are all on our own path to the same destination, and the resources for each of us along the way are infinite. Our hearts know intuitively, that not only are we extremely powerful creators, but that it is all happening in Divine Timing, and the way it is supposed to happen.

As a coach, it is amazing to help others to experience their own version of it. It is like reliving it from the beginning through new eyes, and from a different perspective. What joy!

Here is another fact you may not be aware of: We are all coaches because we teach, guide, and learn from each other at the same time.

How to Raise Your Energy Frequency

Besides thinking a "better feeling" thought, there are a number of different ways to raise our energy frequency, such as:

- Prayer, meditation, practice of BEing in the moment
- Heart coherence

- Gratitude/appreciation, Focus Wheel
- Writing/journaling
- Creative visualization
- Guided imagery
- Singing
- Laughing
- Acting
- Listening to music
- Dancing
- Exercising
- Yoga
- Martial arts
- Massage
- Reading
- Energy work
- Breath work

All of these activities will help to align the head with the heart. It helps us get out of our intellectual mind and into BEing who we really are, a spontaneous fountain of fun and joy. When you are in this space, you are not thinking about who is watching, or wondering what people are saying or thinking. You are not seeking approval outside of yourself, comparing, recognition, applause, reassurance, or needing attention.

You quickly become aware of your vibrational frequency using these techniques with daily practice. Make them healthy habits you repeat. Repetition is the key to understanding and creating a lifestyle that serves you and the greater good:

1. Become aware of how you are feeling. You cannot BE in a space of peace and have negative thoughts.

2. The family pet, infants, and young children are great antennae from outside of yourself to help you detect if you are in a low or high frequency vibration. You will see it in the way they respond to you and your energy.

As a reminder since this is important to understand: A high-energy frequency is not necessarily indicated by hyperactivity, busyness, loudness, talkativeness, or an excitable personality. There are many reasons why someone would exhibit these characteristics, and often it has little to do with heart coherence. A person can be in a high-energy frequency state and be grounded, calm, mild-mannered, humble or at peace.

If we stay at a low-energy level for an extended period of time, we will attract more of it. That is why when our day starts out bad and we dwell on it, instead of flipping the switch and intentionally creating better thoughts, the day gets progressively worse and worse. It's inevitable that the low-energy frequency attracts more of the same. In short, if you are experiencing any emotion that you do not want to experience, deliberately change it by changing your thoughts.

Because everything is energy, including our thoughts, there is no "wrong" energy. It is just different frequencies. Since everything is right, the human brain/mind has difficulty interpreting the words "no," "don't," and "not." Therefore, it translates the statement, "I don't want to be upset," as "I want to be upset." It then gives you more of what you said you wanted, "being upset." Likewise, it is the same for everything else we say we "don't" want.

The quickest way to get to a higher vibration is to reach for a better feeling thought. The list of aforementioned activities are a mechanism or tool, to jumpstart your emotions in the direction of happiness and joy. Then, intentionally do things that bring a higher frequency to you. Be particularly careful of what and whom you bring into your space and the frequency that they bring to you. Each of us must take personal response-ability for the energy we bring into any space.

One great way to do this is to give away that which we desire. For example, if we want more compassion, we wouldn't play victim in order to have people feel sorry for us as we tell our drama/trauma story. Giving compassion to others is circular and in motion, therefore, it in turn will come back to us, and often threefold.

Likewise, always give to yourself everything you are expecting from others: compassion, love, respect, flexibility, support, understanding, goodness, grace, etc.

Focus on what you want to create with Divine Intention. "I am calm and peace," and you will raise your frequency, and in turn, become more calm and peaceful. It really is quite simple, and yet we complicate life by thinking it has to be more complicated. The more we create a simple life, the more we notice how complex we've unintentionally, yet seriously, complicated it.

Affirmations, when done with pure positive intention for the greater good, are a tool to raise your energy frequency. It's not about positive thinking. It is about positive BEingness. Thinking takes place in the head. BEing takes place in the heart. This again is the true meaning of the Law of Attraction.

For example, when we are in a state of positive BEingness, we are in effect, giving it away to others, because we are pulsing that energy out. On the other end of the spectrum, when we are in a state of scarcity, ego, competitiveness, or negativity, we are also giving that away to other people. (At least to people who aren't aware they do not have to own it. After all, if someone tries to give you something and you don't take it, whose is it?) They know it and can feel the negative energy; therefore, we cannot hide or fake it. We are transparent, and wear our intentions on our sleeves. Some people are very aware of it. Others are not, yet they know something seems amiss about the situation. You've heard people state, "Something doesn't feel right; I just cannot put my finger on it."

It is a pulsing energy frequency that they are feeling. We can trust that at the very moment we sense energy coming toward us that doesn't feel that it is serving us, there is something going on with that person at that time. Remember what is going on with them is none of our business. Nor does it mean it is forever, so don't entirely dismiss them from your life. They appeared in your life story for a reason.

That is because it is their stuff, their issue. It is their personal response-ability to do something with it until they raise their own vibration. It means finding a way to do this by:

- Not projecting it onto another person
- Not playing victim
- Not pointing fingers
- Taking personal response-ability for what is created

We cannot do any of these for someone else. It is not someone else's fault, because we create our own reality. We create everything at any given moment based on how we treat others, which is actually a reflection of how we feel about ourselves at any given moment. It is true that the people who treat us the worst are the ones who need to be loved the most. This can be challenging, but we'll learn an easier way as we progress through this book together.

I tread lightly when I use the word "fault." Because in doing so, we tend to imagine that something was a mistake. There are no mistakes. There are only mis-takes as Michael Beckwith teaches. Do another take and get on with it. When we do anything from Divine Intention and someone mis-takes it, what they are seeing is not our stuff; don't own it. It's not yours. Do not take on stuff that isn't yours. You have enough of your own which you will learn to break through in the next chapter.

❤ ❤ ❤

5

HEALING BY BREAKING THROUGH PATTERNS

Do you know why patterns show up in your life? Would you like to learn how to break through them? Keep in mind what you just learned about the true meaning of the Law of Attraction as we explore the following together.

Like many people who are familiar with mainstream's idea of the Law of Attraction, I initially thought that I was attracting all events and people, and that this was happening because my frequency was a match with that event or person. This is not entirely true.

As soon as we declare what we want, and who we are, we will have infinite opportunities to experience the opposite. This happens so that we can more clearly know what it is that we DO want to create and who we really are.

Neale Donald Walsch refers to it as the .Law of Opposites." When you experience the difference or contrast between the two, there are two choices: Continue on the path that you declared to be your truth, or pay attention to the unwanted thing/event you don't want. Your re-action to this unwanted thing/event will play a significant role in the outcome or the reality you create for yourself (and possibly others). Allow me to repeat another important point.

When we have a sudden, extreme re-action, it often catapults into exactly the same thing over and over again. We are literally re-acting. When we "re-act" (hyphenate it between E and A), we are "RE-ACTing." We are replaying the same scene over and over again. In other words, we are repeating action patterns that do not serve us. This is often wasting valuable time and dishonoring oneself.

Incidentally, rearrange the letters in the word REACT and add an E (for Evolve) at the end, and you have the word CREATE! You cannot evolve when you RE-ACT, only when you CREATE!

When we stay focused on the path that we declared to be our truth, it is at that time that we literally break a pattern. The more we practice this technique, the easier it will become. This doesn't mean the other person wins, not at all. It simply means that you care so much about staying focused on what you want to create, that the event in question is not important enough to pull you away. In other words, you maintain your focus. It does not mean you are weak if you do not defend yourself, which is the exact opposite of what most people think. This is true regardless of the situation you are in, and even those situations that you_____. (Fill in the blank with what you think does not apply to your situation.)

Creating anything requires consistent, focused action motorized by passion. You cannot be in the state of passion when you are in re-active mode.

I also want to address a common concern. Some may be thinking, "I understand what you are saying, but I don't want the other person to think they won." What does it matter whether both of you walk away feeling like you won? When you choose to remain focused on who you know that you are, you create what you truly wanted and that was to stay laser focused and not be distracted by drama that did not serve either person. Would you rather make someone wrong or create what you want?

Attempting to make someone wrong is always an illusion, temporary, and a waste of constructive energy. Stay focused on what you can create at a high-energy frequency that will attract more of the same to you. It really is that simple.

Your Truth May Make You Uncomfortable

In fact, it often does. Be aware that there is the probability that you may confuse comfort with your truth. The things that make us uncomfortable are often the very things we need to experience in order to grow.

Another great exercise is to create a list of things that you are resisting. On your "Resistance List," be sure you include absolutely everything you can think of. Usually, the top 10 are the areas in which you feel the most resistance. They are also the areas in which the most growth is needed, and will occur if applied.

Be sure that your resistance list includes things that are nagging at you to step into. These may be things that you need to find the courage to do. They may be recurring to-do thoughts, or someday, maybe I'll do _____ thoughts. Be sure to include those things that even the thought of attempting them, causes some degree of anxiety. Remember, anxiety is an illusion.

One of my resistant list items was putting this book together and making it publicly available. After all, I resisted this for over twenty years! Even as I write this now in the last and eleventh edit, I was procrastinating about finishing it and it was 98% complete. So don't feel bad or beat yourself up. Everyone has something they are procrastinating about.

Most of the items on your list are a step toward your truth, and will undoubtedly make you uncomfortable. Depending on what is on your list, every week or month, I respectfully suggest that you take one of those items and step into it or just let it go. You will feel a huge sense of release. This will create an amazing amount of creative momentum and growth in your personal, spiritual, and emotional life, as well as in your business life. Resistance is simply the illusion of stuck energy that when released, frees up space to create.

There are times when people confuse their truth with being comfortable. They tell themselves and others, that they are comfortable and content with the way their lives are right now. But, are they?

In the words of Neale Donald Walsch, "Are you BEing the greatest grandest version of who you really are?" In order to grow and evolve our spiritual and emotional intelligence, we must get comfortable being uncomfortable. This is because the speed of our growth will depend on our willingness to explore larger degrees of being uncomfortable on our quest for personal development. The term, "growing pains," refers not only to challenging times of growth for a child, student, and/or new business, but to all practices of life.

Is It Really About the Stuff?
As we age, many of us have discovered that living a full life isn't about the material items that we have collected. It is more about HOW that new dress, new car, new house, and so on, makes us "feel."

What we want is the key to what we need to give away in our life, in order to have it ourselves – sometimes in threefold! Allow me to clarify.

When you desire a material item (or experience), and you examine the reason for acquiring it, (which you "think" will give you that feeling), you discover it isn't about that object or experience at all. In fact, the quickest way to get that feeling is not to acquire material things, but to give the experience of that feeling to someone else.

If I want to be uplifted, I will be uplifting to others. If I desire breathing space, I give it to others. If I want clear vision, I hold that space for others. When I do this with Divine Intention, in order to help others, then it will come back to me threefold in ways I do not expect. When I expect it to arrive a certain way and only that way, then I am not open to seeing it arrive in infinitely possible ways, and I will miss it.

When you get to the root of the WHY behind the WHY for anything that you say you want, it will always come down to a feeling or emotion that you desire. You will discover that the feeling involves your desire to be happy and loved. Give that to others and always and in all ways give that to yourself.

What You Desire Outside of You Is What is Needed Inside of You

As previously mentioned (it deserves repetition in order to remember it), we arc all students, as well as teachers at the same time. Therefore, every author writes for themselves, as well as others. This means that there is not a "special few" who are capable of teaching. Everyone teaches and everyone learns. We often teach what we need to learn.

Because we have a limited ability to express our thoughts and emotions in human words, it is sometimes a challenge to know when spirit is in-spiring (in spirit) us. Sometimes we do not trust what we are getting. It feels like a fleeting thought and we instantly dismiss it. Over the years I have learned to listen and trust spirit and take a leap of faith when I get a Divine nudge.

When we ignore those God winks or Divine nudges, they become more and more persistent, because, "What we resist will persist." Many people feel called to do many things, but do not honor that calling or themselves, in the process. It is only when we stop to really listen with our heart, and then act on it, that we put into motion what is Divine Intention.

We want to pay attention to what our emotions are telling us and how we are feeling. The desire for a particular item or experience outside of us is not what it's all about. It IS always about what's going on INSIDE of us. When we honor ourselves by trusting in our inner Divine Knowing, we are opening ourselves to our truth.

Someone else may have a similar goal or desire as you do, but spirit could have a totally different "spiritually intelligent" reason for they're creating it in their respective life. Consequently, their spirit may be sending them this need to "experience" these emotions for a completely different reason. You know instinctively at all times, what is best for you. You just have to "remember." Listen to your heart wisdom - your spiritual intelligence.

It is all about the emotion involved, so when you get the positive charge of the emotion behind it, the result is passion. When you have passion, you will create momentum so fast that keeping up with yourself is the key. One of my favorite questions is, "Are you keeping up with you?"

The reason we desire experiences is the same underlying reason that we desire material items. It is all about the "feeling" that is created when we have the experience. Everyone will have different reasons or a WHY behind the WHY. Again, there is no wrong reason.

To make this clearer, here is an example: When I visited Egypt in the late 1990s, it symbolized an opening of my heart and mind. I found something far greater than me, and a far bigger sense of love energy. This is because I was willing to go beyond my previous thought programming to discover the mysteries that I didn't know about our world.

However, I found that I already had the answer. I didn't need to go thousands of miles away to find it, although the trip was life changing to experience the contrast of a different culture. There was no need to go anywhere outside of myself, because it resided within me. It became clear that I already have everything that I needed then and in the future. All that was left to do was to remember it, take a leap of faith, and follow my heart.

When we all follow what our spiritual intelligence tells us to do, no one is left out, for it is always for the greater good of all. Wouldn't this world be an amazing place to live in if everyone adopted that as our mantra? There would be no need for wars, competition, politics as we know it today, or division. It would simply BE what Jesus, and many other Ascended Masters, intended this world to BE. What all of them taught us was The Golden Rule.

The world I speak of is possible, as anything is possible. We are putting a cap on our creative power when we limit our thinking by labeling it as a fantasy or pipe dream. There is an infinite supply of everything for everyone. That is the universal plan. When you know and understand this, you will no longer need to feel combative, competitive, better than someone else, or any other emotion that does not serve the greater good. You will go about your life BEing who you are, and encouraging others to do the same. This is choosing to use your power, while allowing everyone to use his or hers. Could this be the missing link to truly connecting to others on a deeper level? Are your ready to explore it?

❤ ❤ ❤

6

CO-OPERATION
& CO-CREATION

Our bodies are made of the same biological matter, as well as being energy, which means we are not only biologically but also spiritually connected. Yet, we are all individuals; therefore, we actually have the best of both worlds.

Imagine a tree blowing in the wind and the branches are naturally touching each other. The tree is one large, living-breathing object. The branches, twigs, bark, and leaves are all part of the whole. Humanity is the same way - all being part of the whole, and thereby connected. When space gets a little tight for the tree, the branches and leaves seek to reach beyond to find their own space in a fellowship of co-operation and co-creation.

Yet, when things don't go our way, we as humans, take drastic measures to force" the issue. We are in opposition or suppression, rather than trying to create a win-win solution so that we each find our own space, have room to grow, and at the same time respect the space of others.

In keeping with the tree metaphor, humans tend to pull out all the weapons they've ever learned, thereby pruning their tree in an unhealthy manner, in an attempt to overpower the other "twig." Imagine a tree doing such a thing. It would not last long. Neither will the human race, if we continue in the same destructive, competitive patterns. Wouldn't it be better to find a win-win alternative so that everyone has abundance, rather than fighting to gain power over another? There IS plenty of abundance to go around.

There is also enough power to go around to allow every individual person to feel important, needed, loved, and secure. We can empower others by giving them back their control so that they can choose in a co-operative and co-creative environment. Isn't it easier and better for all when we are given the ability to choose within a co-operative environment without consequences attached?

Instead of trying to beat someone and eliminate the competition, why not BE a Divine Visionary and lead in a new way of heart-felt thought and action? Our society has many amazing visionaries who separate themselves from their peers for various reasons. How wonderful a world we could live in, if these incredible souls formed together in a space of heartfelt co-operation in order to create a better world. Together they could find a co-creative way to make it work so we can have co-operative power with one another. There are a number of organizations that have been formed to help raise this awareness. Would you be willing to join us in creating a world that serves all? Reference the resource section for more information at: www.BEingSpirituallyIntelligent.com.

Most of mainstream society is unaware of what some large corporations and small businesses will do, or spare no expense in time or money, to eliminate what they perceive as a competitor. Could their resources, time, and energy be better invested in making the world a better place for all? For example, there was an article in *YES Magazine*, about a telecommunications company (February 2012 edition) spending nine times the money they would have spent on business improvements, in order to attempt to wipe out their biggest competitor! It didn't work.

There is only one race. It is called the human race. When will the human race wake up? Will it be too late when we do? How much damage will be done to our health, environment, communities, economy, and the quality of life by that time?

For those who think this is fantasy and not a possible reality of the world we live in, there are cultures today, and throughout history, that chose to co-create and live in co-operation with each other instead of competition. Imagine how much better everyone would feel, knowing they're needs will be met. Our stress would be reduced considerably and our health would immediately improve. Would you believe our physical and mental health is really all about how well we learn to manage stress? Stress is simply the illusion of being stuck and it starts with our thoughts.

You may debate that healthy competition creates growth and motivates people. The mere use of the phrase is an oxymoron. The issue with healthy competition is that it motivates a person based on something that is outside of him or her self. When that happens, it cloaks their inherent power from them. It confuses them, and they begin to think that they must prove to themselves and others that they have value and worth.

Furthermore, they begin to think that there must be winners and losers, thereby creating a scarcity mentality. Would it not be better for all to create a win-win situation that both sides can enjoy? When you make it about someone's value or worth, the results are always short term. This is because you distract them from their personal power and make them dependent on you, others, or sources outside of them for everything they think they need.

Looking outside of oneself for motivation will always bring short-term results. For example, when someone's full attention is on the external, such as how they look, they are basing their worth and value on the opinion of others. Furthermore, because we all think and do things differently, we are all in a totally different space. No one knows or can imagine, what it is like to walk in the shoes of another.

When this happens, people acquire an addictive dependency on acknowledgment, acceptance, and recognition. The business world often considers it to be an asset in building a successful business when, in fact, it is manipulative and dysfunctional to disempower the very people that are the business' true assets. It does not encourage them to be their best for the greater good of all. So, what does that mean? When we are at our personal best, we affect others in a positive manner. That is why closing your mind and heart, holding yourself back, and not living in your truth (which is your full potential), is like holding back the butterfly effect of positive experiences for everyone.

Remember, external appearances do not make people who they are, and are merely distractions and temporary fixes. This usually indicates that something much deeper is going on. Whatever it is does not serve the greater good of all.

Do not confuse "looking good" with "feeling good." Which is more important to you? When given a choice, most people would choose feeling good. Someone could be unhealthy physically and/or mentally and look great, and at the same time be depressed, unhappy, and anxious. In addition, remember that each person's definition of looking and feeling good will be different.

Many cultures outside of the United States (which we, as westerners, see as not as advanced), consider beauty to be in a person's soul and spirit. In other words, a person's Divine Intention and passion to connect with other people is what is most important to them. I am beginning to see westerners BEcome more spiritually connected in recent years and that is exciting!

Connecting with others is not about enabling someone with pity. It is about <u>sincere</u> empathy. When you connect with someone on a soul level, you are listening to their heart, instead of just hearing them. Hearing is a process that works biologically through the organs and bones of the ear using vibrations. When you are listening to someone you are connecting with them on a much deeper level than hearing, and they will know it.

Natural Leadership in Everyday Life and Business

There are many books on leadership that contain each person's perspective of what leadership <u>should</u> look like and what a leader does. There are as many definitions of leadership as there are people who do or do not proclaim to be leaders.

There is a common underlying principle in all leadership themed books. This principle focuses on connecting to people, as opposed to the only goal being financial gain. This underlying principle is the foundation for all spiritual and religious books too, including the Bible. That principle again, comes back to *The Golden Rule*. As long as we are always aware of what we do unto others, as we would want done unto us, leadership comes natural. We will attract people without worrying that we are leading them correctly. Leadership is so simple, and yet we make it so complicated that we reserve this seemingly special state of BEing for only a few.

I am guessing you "feel" a spark of truth in these written words. Some people reading this may deny it. That is because society has conditioned many to think "left-brained," and through EGO.

We have an innate ability to read (or feel) our parents energy when we are born. In fact, we are better at it the younger we are, than as we age. The older we get, the more we are taught to ignore our intuition, which interferes with our natural gifts. We often learn without even realizing it, a person's true intentions. We can feel/sense it, whether we wish to acknowledge it or not.

Therefore, it is natural that those who can lead with compassion and connect with others, are followed. This is because they are attracted to the energy that is naturally within all of us. It is also quite common for people with natural leadership skills to not only be followed, but also sometimes copied (either publicly, subtly, or secretly) by others, because they are attracted to a natural leader's grounded authenticity.

The natural leader, who has the highest purpose in mind, generally does not beat the "I am a leader, follow me" drum. They will often intentionally move away from the limelight and work behind the scenes. This is because their focus is about wanting to do what they know is their calling. Furthermore, they do not feel the need to spend time attempting to convince others of their leadership abilities. In fact, they don't see it that way at all and it doesn't even occur to them. Although it may be flattering when others follow, they rarely look for confirmation from others that they are on the right path. They know on a deep spiritual level who they are, what they want to create, and so they follow their heart based on their own core values.

Here is the news you've been waiting for: We are ALL natural-born leaders. Some of us have forgotten who we are and why we are here.

Follow or Lead

Have you ever met someone who wouldn't hesitate to shame, blame/guilt, intimidate, humiliate, or manipulate someone? Why do they do it? This is usually done simply as a means to create a temporary sense of leverage to get what they want. Never mind the effects of how it will make the other person feel. How often has that turned out the way they wanted long term?

Wouldn't it be simpler to discover a win-win solution together based on a trusting relationship?

In case you are thinking, "Hey, it is a dog eat dog world out there; I will never give in to anyone. I'm right. You must be out of your mind to think this way. This kind of thinking is most certainly the way to get killed and eaten by the competition."

I would respond by saying, "Thank you for noticing I am not in my mind. I am in my heart." If enough people courageously chose what they know in their own hearts to be true, we could create a new world based on love and compassion for everyone.

The question is, are we using the terms "follow and lead" appropriately? Will you follow the masses that are projecting the illusion of having the "one-up," power-over mentality? The easy way out is to follow someone who appears to have it together, even though we know in our heart it is not necessarily in our best interest.

Or will you have the courage to truly lead a few who know that it doesn't take many to create a shift in human consciousness (mindset)? True leadership is about leading everyone with no one intentionally left out. This also means never intentionally doing anything that might make someone feel less than.

You've heard the term, "When the student is ready the teacher will appear." This is only one definition or understanding of what that means. We teach and we learn, often at the same time. There is no shame, nor is there anything taken away from a person's leadership to admit it. A top executive can learn from anyone, and he/she who are willing to be vulnerable and admit it with ease, confidence, and grace, steps into his/her heart and truly leads from the inside out. Therein is a trust formed, so strong that it is unshakeable.

We Are All Entrepreneurs on a Spiritual Level
While I have a passion for working with and helping business entrepreneurs be heard and create what they want, I also love their visionary/creative ideas, flair for life, their ability and confidence to create anything at any time, their forward focus, and their zest to do what they love. Did you know we are all spiritual entrepreneurs?

The following are a few definitions of the word, "entrepreneur":

1. A person who organizes and manages any enterprise, especially a business, usually with considerable initiative and risk.
2. An employer of productive labor; contractor.
3. The owner or manager of a business enterprise who, by risk and initiative, attempts to make profits.

Let's look at these definitions from a soul or spirit's perspective. Every day, with each decision and choice we make, we organize and manage our own personal enterprise with considerable initiative and we take risks. We are all employers of our own labors of life, creating spiritual contracts through our connections with others. Isn't all of life a risk that results in profits of some type?

There are times when we choose to play small and hold back our natural talents and individuality. This is because of the imagined FEAR (False Evidence Appearing Real) that we create as a distraction. Our hearts will tell us something different, if we will only listen.

A successful business entrepreneur wears many hats, and juggles a lot of different activities in order to create a profit. At the same time, they are helping others stay purposely focused in order to get what they each want.

Is that what you are creating for yourself and others as a spiritual entrepreneur? The level at which we are willing to explore our true potential and stay focused in the direction of creating it is BEing Spiritually Intelligent. This determines our level of peace and happiness; both in self and in those we teach and learn from.

Did you realize that you are an important part of the whole picture? Just like each element of an artist's painting is important to the overall outcome of the painting, you are too. Everyone is here for a specific reason.

Are you willing to explore your purpose with me now and take a look at how you are showing up so far in the Divine's painting of life? It may be a bit uncomfortable but as we have learned so far, staying comfortable doesn't create. Nothing happens until something moves.

❤❤❤

7

HOW WE AFFECT OTHERS

How do you think people are affected when we have Divine Intentions toward them? How does that energy feel to them? In contrast, what if we don't have the best of intentions in mind?

They know it, sense it, and feel it, but they may not express it. The interesting thing is that people fear "fear." Yes, that is typed correctly. When you know that someone has a reputation of not being nice, exploding with anger, being disruptive, self-centered or gossiping, it is a fact that others do not want to be around that kind of low-frequency energy. However, they won't want them on their bad side either, because they don't want the wrath of dysfunction targeting them. No one wants that kind of drama disrupting his or her life.

People who enjoy drama usually know it. This method is a manipulative way to get what they want. It is very much like a small child having a temper tantrum. Children will try many ways to seek to manipulate their parents, until they determine what works best. It is a learned process. These children are not necessarily wrong. They just don't know any other way to survive, yet that is.

When these children grow into adulthood, but have still not outgrown/overcome it, problems ensue. Because they never learned how to deal with situations that do not serve their egos, they don't understand the win-win power of cooperation. When these adults have great power over others, it's so scary that people don't want to upset them. Therefore, they go along with them on a superficial level, at least until they can find a way to remove themselves gracefully and unnoticed. This is the very thing that eventually brings down families, friendships, communities, businesses, small companies, big corporations, cities, countries, and even nations. Through out history, even if it has worked temporarily, it is not a real connection. Those in influential positions, who do not know how to handle the power of authority, will often abuse their right to that power. People may pretend to be their friend, because they are afraid of them, or fear the power they think they hold over others.

In extreme cases, those caught up in this low-frequency energy, sometime resort to drastic measures. Sometimes the only way they know how to survive is to meet conflict with firearms in a forceful, aggressive, greedy, and an inhumane way. You've heard the sayings, "dog eat dog," and "kill or be killed." Unfortunately, they simply don't realize that there is a totally different way of thinking, BEing and doing. It is one that will create a much more positive environment, in which all others can live, and everyone has enough of what they need.

There is a name for an organism that takes more than it can use or needs. It's greedy, forceful, and aggressive. It is called "cancer." Until we realize that co-operation and co-creation is the answer, instead of violence, we are like a cancer to others and Mother Earth.

I am not referring to a physical/biological cancer within a body, but to the emotional cancers within all of us. The subject of cancer and other ailments in the body are a whole other book; one in which we would learn the effects of our emotional conditions and stresses on the physical body. My intent here, however, is to:

- Raise your awareness of what you do want.
- Assist you in taking personal response-ability for where you are right now in your life. Until you do that, and make peace with it, you cannot move forward. Pointing fingers outside of self and blaming others, serves no one.
- Help you remember that you had the power all along. All you have to do is look within instead of looking outside of yourself for confirmation or permission.

You are looking outside of yourself, if you resort to any of these scenarios:

- Making someone wrong because either they don't think the way that you do, have the same interests that you do, or don't do something the exact same way that you do. This mindset is really you looking into a mirror at yourself and saying, "I am not accepting you as who you really are." People are our mirrors.
- In order for you to feel good in this time-space physical moment, you feel the need to compare yourself to something or someone outside of you.
- Wondering if another person is doing something better than you, is more attractive than you, more successful, more powerful, happier, having more fun, has more friends, and so on. When you compare, you are always making someone or something wrong. This is a big red flag that you are creating division within yourself and with others.
- Obsessively telling others your victim stories.
- Attracting attention so others feel sorry for you or think highly of you.

What if we decided to be a more highly evolved species that accepted people, situations and circumstances for what they are? There would be peace in knowing that everything is happening just as we chose it. There is always something to learn from any situation. It's about finding the pearl in each situation and moving forward to re-create our life.

Stepping Out of the Box

Let's explore a statement: What we believe about almost everything could possibly be and probably is, inaccurate.

May I suggest we look at our beliefs about the way things are from a new perspective. Obviously, with all of the problems we are having today in our social, financial, political, educational, as well as health-related structures, something is not working. Looking back on history, it is a cycle that repeats itself. It will continue to repeat itself unless or until, we break that re-action chain which has not served us in a very long time. Clearly, these last few years have reinforced the urgency of our need to make long overdue changes.

The questions are: How can we improve our system so that everyone in the world can have enough food, clothing, power, or money? How can we ensure that everyone in the world has a happy life and feels loved?

We look at cultures where people live in huts with dirt floors and we see them as poor; yet they are happier than most westerners. Their happiness comes from a deep soul level. This is because they are connected to who they really are and they are enjoying life as it is. They are not worried about whether someone is more prosperous, happier, more attractive, etc. Nor do they care what others think. They don't question whether or not they could be more loving, because they ARE loving. They don't question whether they are happy, because they ARE happy.

Happiness is not something that you declare. It is something that you are BEing. It's not something that is to be made into a competition. Competitiveness is low-frequency thinking. Low frequency thinking can be defined as looking outside of one's self for approval or confirmation, by comparing what we do or say to what other people are doing or saying. We are then making someone wrong or less than, in an attempt to make ourselves feel better.

When you are BEing _____ (Fill in the blank), you know it. You don't question it or compare it to anything outside of yourself. You don't even think about doing it. When you KNOW anything, it IS your truth. It's who you are. For example, I know my eyes are brown in the light that a human eye can see. I don't go around comparing my eye color to others to convince myself of it. I'm not obsessing over it by looking outside of myself and talking about it to other people. I wouldn't question it if someone told me my eyes were green. I would simply smile, and perhaps think to myself, "that's interesting," and move on.

When we compare anything, we create division whether we know it or not. We make something less than or wrong. This is often referred to as competition. Even what some term, "healthy competition," will create some form of dysfunctional division. Over time, dysfunctional division collapses the entire system. Again, this is exactly what we are seeing now in society's systems: finances, education, health, business, politics, etc.

When division is created, sides are formed. Everyone wants the same things: happiness, love, and security. Why not help each other to acquire it, especially since there already is an unlimited amount for everyone?

In many cultures, competitive thinking is considered low-frequency energy, completely dysfunctional, and a mental health disorder. Whoa! Many people on this planet consider the very thing we thought was a healthy way of life, socially acceptable, taught to our children, and glorified, to be a mental illness. Yet, that is what we declare to be the best and strongest characteristics to embody. The definition would, of course, be different for each person depending on who they are, their situation, and perspective on life.

In the animal kingdom it may appear to be "survival of the fittest," yet most animals don't kill for sport. They kill for food in order to fuel their bodies and physically survive.

Yes, people have different definitions of fun and again, my intention is not to make anyone wrong. What I am proposing is that we as a society take a step back and really look at our life. Instead of declaring, "I am having more success, more fun, more power," take a look at what you are doing. How is it affecting others and impacting the world we live in? What everyone else is doing doesn't matter. When you look outside of yourself for confirmation and compare yourself to someone else, you are not confident in who you are. This means you are depending on something or someone else outside of yourself for that confirmation. All that you think you need you already have; you must simply choose to use it.

When you are grounded and very clear about who you are and why you are here, then none of that will matter. That's Divine Confidence!

Trust & Dis-Trust

Trust is an incredibly powerful 5-letter word that is the foundation of all relationships, and does not pertain only to our small circle of family, friends, neighbors and pets. It is also very important in business relationships with clients, staff, supervisors, employers, employees and most importantly, trusting ourselves.

When trust does not exist in a relationship, nothing will grow. Think of the 5-letters in the word trust as the five important components to effectively cause something to grow. Trust is the 1) seed, 2) soil, 3) water, 4) sunshine, and 5) fertilizer.

Trust is an interesting word because it can grow organically. You are either moving toward more trust or less trust. It spreads like a virus, which is not always a bad thing. When we talk about things going viral on the Internet, it is usually a good thing. It helps people to grow and learn in some way.

Whatever frequency you are vibrating at, or causing in your actions and intentions, will result in either trust or dis-trust. Dis-trust will cause dis-ease, which will in turn, affect a relationship. This is the opposite of what you desire to create, *unless it isn't.*

As soon as trust breaks down, even if it was not intentional, it is important to re-establish it. While it is true that some people do not want to trust, we must realize that it is their choice. We cannot control what people say or how they feel about us, or even what they do to us. That is because it's not about us. What they see in us is what they do not like about themselves. Perhaps they see in us something that they feel they lack, resulting in what is commonly referred to as envy. Envy is a fear-based word and an illusion. Remember, no one lacks anything. We all have everything we need.

Furthermore, those who see in themselves what they are unable to tolerate in someone else, knowingly or unknowingly, put up a wall of resistance, and often become angry, violent, vengeful or depressed. They will repeat this pattern until they acknowledge and accept that part of themselves that has the characteristics of another they are judging to be wrong.

If we are honest, we all recognize something in ourselves, at one time or another that created some kind of emotional baggage that still lies within our cellular memory. We fear that those negative experiences in our memory banks (depending on the meaning we apply to it) are happening or will happen again.

We are all messengers. Some people are simply more aware of it than others right now. All of us operate as human radio frequency antennae. Humankind would remember that sooner if we paid closer attention to ourselves (instead of pointing out what we consider the faults of others), and aligned our hearts and minds with what we intuitively know.

Which is the Right Reality & Version of God?

What if we opened our hearts to the possibility that everyone's reality and version of God was right? Furthermore, if we honored their truth, that is, what was right for "them" at any given time, imagine the world we could live in. As an example analogy, consider that if there is a distant city that is our destination, there are multiple routes to get there. So in a sense, we are merely each choosing our own route.

What if we introduced the same concept into all other areas of our life by looking at all that is not working in our world today? We continually resist bringing spiritual intelligence into our businesses, our schools, our politics, and on and on. When we make others wrong and create division, the foundational structure deteriorates.

❤ ❤ ❤

8

WHOLESOME
WELL-BEING

One of the first steps in changing your life is to **recreate WHOLEsome health and well-BEing.** To be truly healthy, it is important to progress toward a balance of mind, body, spirit, and emotion. This will in effect balance all of the energy centers (chakras) of the body. Without our health, we often do not feel we have the energy to focus on other areas of our life. The body is an amazing tool that can be sculpted into whatever we choose so that we are able to live the life we were meant to in order to create our purpose.

Side Note: Balance is a word that is commonly misunderstood by many people, as it appears to be an outcome that is unattainable and therefore is disregarded as important. This is because pure balance all the time is unattainable. It's not about reaching the destination. It is about in-joying the process of the adventure.

Of course, as humans, none of us are perfect. We all have our idiosyncrasies and addictions. Yes, some addictions are currently more socially accepted by mainstream society than others. Like the rest of humanity, I still experience some struggle from time to time based on my choices even though I let go of a significant amount of body weight and emotional baggage years ago. However, the process was a tremendous learning experience to move through. For this I am forever grateful, because what I have learned about WHOLEsome health and well-BEing has given me the skills to continue my path of purpose with renewed passion. I am also able to help others when they decide to choose to live a lifestyle of abundant health, hope and happiness.

Energy Frequencies in Food and Water

Personal experience and listening to my body helped me realize the difference between the higher vibrational energy that is within the food and water that we consume, versus the lower vibrational energy in other things we consume. Low vibrational foods include junk foods that are filled with sugar, fat, and empty carbohydrates that have little to no nutritional value. Unhealthy, low vibrational foods put our bodies into a nutritional deficit, thus depleting us of nutrients. I soon learned that the quality of our food depends on its energy vibration, and that has a direct impact on how we feel.

Would you be surprised to learn that this includes our water? There have been many scientific experiments done that document the molecular structure of water from the tap vs. water that has been blessed with Divine Intention. In fact, if you look at both types of frozen water crystals with a microscope, they will look totally different. The water that is blessed with Divine Intention has an attractive geometric pattern, as if you were looking through a kaleidoscope! To find out more, read "The Hidden Messages in Water," by Masaru Emoto. It is incredibly interesting to know that "any of us" can change the molecular structure of water, because we choose to have the Divine Intention to do so.

Why did Jesus bless water, wine, and food? Do we only say grace before meals to show thanks, or are we also doing it to bless the food with Divine Intention, thereby changing the molecular structure? The frequency of our foods and beverages directly affect how we feel – which we now know is critically important to make better choices and create a healthier lifestyle.

Loving & Appreciating Yourself
We already have within us the means to love and appreciate ourselves. You will come to realize, just as I

have, that everything that has happened to us in the past has created the person we are today. Granted, there may have been times we felt that what happened didn't serve us. However, it does serve to illustrate the extreme contrast between what we have and what we want to create now. It also allows us to appreciate even more, who we really are.

For me personally, just when I thought I couldn't love myself more, I discovered I do. Just when I thought I couldn't appreciate myself more, I discovered I could. Isn't it a wonderful feeling to know that you can do this too?

What about the not so good things that happen, that cause us to question the path we are on? It could be the death of a loved one, losing a job or relationship, perhaps an illness or a crime that happened to a loved one. When things happen that we feel we have no control over, we often ask, why us? How could these bad things happen to good people? As time passes, and we take care to keep an open mind and heart, time heals wounds so that the WHY becomes clearer in the greater, grander creation of things.

Whatever the event, it was simply a catalyst for us to create a pivotal point. As previously mentioned, we are constantly being called to step into our next grandest action. You know this in your heart, but sometimes it shows up as resistance and procrastination.

It is okay if when we are called to do something, we choose to ignore it. Since we have free will, it is our choice. However, we will continue to get gentle Divine nudges; in fact, unlimited numbers of them. Some of those Divine nudges may be people who show up in our life as we go about our day.

The person behind you at the grocery store that you choose to ignore may be the perfect person who has the answer you are seeking in your life at that particular time. Are you choosing to resist talking or acknowledging that person for one reason or another? Example: Had you talked with them, you may have discovered in casual conversation that they are involved in a business that needs someone with your qualifications, and was exactly what your heart is calling you to do. Therefore, it is a missed opportunity for both of you. This is another way in which our actions, or in this case, inactions affect others and ourselves.

Let's look at it another way: The person in front of you in line at that same grocery store that you could have spoken with (perhaps they said they liked your jacket), was the person who would have introduced you to the love of your life. (You know, the one you have been waiting to share the rest of your life with!) Do you see another missed opportunity to connect? When you get the feeling to say something to someone, or do something nice for someone, do it without running it through your mind to analyze it. This is your heart leading you.

You will continue to get these gentle Divine nudges. When you step into them, you will discover what is often referred to as "God Winks." Will you notice them or will you pass them off as coincidences or random disconnected thoughts? Your choice to connect or not will create your energy frequency, which in turn, will attract more of the same frequency to you.

What would happen if you chose to change your mindset, and it "in deed" changed your life? Sure, you might lose a little bit of unhealthy EGO, but as we've learned, EGO is "Edging God Out."

Imagine the infinite possibilities that will open up to you. There is a whole other world out there ready for you to see. That is, when you are ready to see it with your heart and not your head. We often do not realize that we are intentionally limiting ourselves with belief systems that no longer serve anyone.

When we open our minds and hearts a bit, we realize that there are many pearls and nuggets of truth contained herein. Imagine how your life will change, when you begin creating whatever you want, however you want it, and as quick as you want it in your world today.

To put it bluntly, if you take the contents herein as impossible for you, it will be. If you see it as huge potential, and put what you have learned into practice, that is what you will create.

Remember, your thoughts create your intentions; the choice you make will create your experience. Your experience is pulsating out into the world as an energy frequency. This attracts more of the same frequency to you, until you raise your frequency from the inside. Thinking negatively will attract more negative relationships and experiences. You in effect get in your own way or pave a path farther away from your highest self. If the path you choose isn't a path of the heart, choose again.

Worry, Anxiety, Depression & Other Dis-Ease

Anything that does not feel good is often the result of how we are thinking, and our perspective of that thought, *unless it isn't*. Perhaps you have heard the saying, "Worrying is using your imagination to create something that you don't want." The majority of illnesses originate from the illusion of stuck energy in the body. Therefore, worrying is using your imagination or your creative abilities to create something that you don't want in your life.

When you look to the past or at something you don't want, you feel you cannot move forward to create what you do want. In thought, as in three-dimensional physical form, two things cannot occupy the same space at the same time. In other words, you cannot think about what you want to create and what you don't want at the same time. Attempting to do so results in depression and the feeling of being stuck. Do you want to alleviate your depression? Take consistent forward action; it empowers! Dwelling in the past causes depression. Dwelling in the future causes anxiety. What you are thinking right NOW creates your future. Right NOW is the gift and that is why it is called the present. Choose your present with spiritual intelligence.

When driving and looking forward, you move forward. If you look off to the side, you often move in the direction you are looking. Certainly, if you are looking in the rear view mirror, you are not going to be able to move forward very effectively. In fact, you will eventually have to come to a complete stop if you continue to focus on what is behind you, or you WILL crash. It is the same in life.

This is really important to know, when you are intending to create positive experiences in your life. Continually focusing on past negative feelings or events, does not allow you to fully let go of the past. It is impossible to create something new, if you are comparing it to a previous experience that may or may not have worked or be related to the situation now. In fact, most of the time it is not.

Living in the Heart Space
There are four inspiring quotations by Ram Dass (www.RamDass.org) that I would like to share with you at this time. They are all expressions of living from your heart. It gives us an idea of what that looks like, as

well as why and how we are holding ourselves back:

1. "The quieter you become, the more that you can hear."

2. "As long as you have certain desires about how it ought to be, you cannot see how it is."

3. "The heart surrenders everything to the moment. The mind judges and holds back."

4. "In most of our human relationships, we spend much of our time reassuring one another that our costumes of identity are on straight."

These quotations reinforce the awareness that we are spiritual beings of light energy having a human experience. That human experience is a costume, a biological human body made of bone, tissue, and blood, which is mostly water. All of which are forms of energy.

What is even clearer is that as we wear this costume, we are seeking admiration, acceptance, approval, or acknowledgement from sources outside of ourselves, that our costume is okay. Wouldn't it be more fulfilling to look and live from within our heart space to know that we are all okay?

When you do, instead of thinking that life is happening to you, it will become clear that it is actually happening through you. You will then be able to learn from these experiences and move forward.

The wonderful thing about these quotations is that they clearly put into perspective that none of us are living our lives fully. This is evident in the fact that as humans, we only use a small percentage of our brain capacity. Scientists has proven this fact, but do not yet know why.

Anything is possible, if we are open to it, and desire it for the greater good of all. Sometimes it is the fear or resistance to changing one or more of our belief systems, that holds us back. When our present belief systems are not creating the results we desire, then something must be changed in order to produce different results that we do desire.

There is "in deed" wisdom contained in the old saying, "The definition of insanity is doing the same thing over and over again and expecting different results." That is entirely true, but most of us do it every day without tweaking it a little bit to see how different the results will be. Rest assured that when we let go of beliefs or mind-game programs that run in our head, all things change.

This does not mean that we need to remain vulnerable or open to low-frequency energy at all times. We put into place a Divine Shield of Protection, by standing in our grounded-ness, checking in with our internal radar of knowing, and living our truth with Divine Intention. At the same time, we remain open to the possibility that there is much more than we are aware of.

Once we all accept these truths and put them into practice, it will create the necessary shift for society that will be the pivotal point we have been waiting for. It will create a co-operative living environment for everyone. Many spiritual leaders call this a "time shift" because massive amounts of people will become aware of who they are and live their own unique truth.

This means we can choose to create whatever world we want. For example, the health care system has been broken for many years. It has now reached the point that people are beginning to take a closer look not only at how they can contribute, but take personal response-ability for their own health. The same applies to their finances. Although most Americans are living far beyond their means, there is plenty to go around. The world would be closer to BEing in balance and at peace if everyone knew they had enough of everything they needed or wanted.

The key is to stop comparing ourselves to the Jones. The Jones are in extreme debt, and hiding their unhappiness behind 'stuff' that has created an image of smoke and mirrors. They are often attempting to impress people they don't even like! They have not yet discovered what you are learning about and how BEing Spiritually Intelligent can change everything.

Our planet is moving into a shift of higher conscious awareness. It is happening now and has been happening for a few years. I'm sure you have noticed that it was happening at lightning speed as we moved through 2012.

In summary, the great news is we get to choose what kind of new world (or new earth) we want. Do we want to continue to fight, kill, maim, and have an imbalance of power? That mindset has not worked for us thus far. Do we really want to recreate the past yet again? Wouldn't it be a better use of our time, energy and resources, to choose to create a more spiritually evolved society? Would it make more sense to cultivate and teach heart coherence to our children and grandchildren (who are the future leaders)?

Throughout millennia, humanity has been waiting for someone to save us. Yes, there have been many prophets and Ascended Masters, but what WE have been waiting for all along, is for US to collectively wake up and take personal response-ability. This must be done individually and collectively to create a new earth based on love, respect, and co-operation.

❤ ❤ ❤

9

OUR RE-ACTIONS
TO THE UNEXPLAINABLE

As far back as I can remember, I have always had an interest in Ancient Egypt. In 1998, my husband and I toured the area of the Great Pyramids and Sphinx. It was at that time that I felt my heart opening, far beyond what my mind could comprehend.

I also realized that there are basically two types of people that go to Egypt:

1) People who feel drawn in some unexplained way.
2) People who are curious because it is the trendy thing to do.

The second type has a common experience when seeing the Giza Pyramids. They experience them as a big pile of rocks. Could these people have closed off their minds and hearts so much that they cannot see beyond what the left side of their brain demands that they see? In other words, they are not seeing beyond the obvious: the incredible engineering of these structures, the broad scope of the pyramids' origin, and what it all means for humanity. This is not a judgment but a simple observation.

I use the Great Pyramids only as an example because this re-action to the unexplainable shows up in many ways.

Visiting the Great Pyramids was a pivotal point in both of our lives. I went searching for answers, but as mentioned earlier, when I returned, I found that I already had the answers. I simply was not allowing myself to open my heart to see the power that I truly had within me.

Although there are many places on our planet that are unexplainable, the majority of the planet's human race chooses to close their mind and heart to anything that cannot be proven or explained. With your heart open, you are willing to let go of a belief system that is not, or is no longer serving you on a grander scale. When you see the unexplainable (such as the pyramids) and are open to seeing beyond the obvious, or what you want to see out of comfort, there is no doubt that these original structures were not built by humans alone, or at least humans that we know of now or throughout our documented historical past.

We have incredible modern technology, lasers, and heavy equipment that are used to build our skyscrapers of iron, steel, and other strong materials. However, we still cannot produce a structure as perfectly level, geometrical, or as mathematically balanced as the Giza Pyramids of Egypt. However, most of mainstream society resists recognizing the wonders of this planet's unexplainable places, like the Giza Pyramids, simply because it does not fit within their comfort zone of what they know.

It seems once again an appropriate place to insert this reminder. We cannot grow individually (and therefore collectively) if we are not willing to step outside of our comfort zone. Just a little step at a time is all that is needed to begin to create growth. The larger the step we take, the larger the growth we create.

It has been said that the Great Pyramid was originally covered with 144,000 mirror-smooth casing stones approximately 20 tons each. The smoothness of these stones was equal to or greater than that of our modern reading glasses. The space between the stones is smaller than a human hair and is exact to the thousandths of an inch. According to Wikipedia, today's modern technology can move stones 10 to 20 tons each only within one or two inches of each other. Consider for a moment, that the height of just one stone is shoulder high and that the Great Pyramid is currently 449-1/2 feet high. The original height is estimated to be 481 feet. The base of the Great Pyramid is one of the largest structures in the world covering more than 13.5 square acres.

That being said, today's scientists' rational explanation is that the Ancient Egyptians used granite quarries located many miles away and pulled those tons and tons of huge stones miles to the Giza plateau using armies of Egyptian men. Is this man's way of justifying his arrogance? Or is there something about our history that we don't want to know or don't want others to know?

Is it a limiting belief to think that the ancient Egyptians carved the stones by hand with picks and handmade axes? Could they have made them perfectly smooth and mathematically balanced with their primitive tools? Could this limited mindset be holding us back from evolving far beyond where our technology is currently?

Another interesting fact is that the three pyramids line up with the Orion solar system and a duplicate set of them has recently been discovered on Mars. Isn't that delightful food for thought?

What did the Egyptians know that we with all of today's technology do not know? There are many theories. However, we have billions of people who are not willing to let go of their present belief systems, which do not serve society's evolution. It is safer for them to continue to think "inside the box." They refuse to question modern day science and the form of history that is being taught to our children in schools. Is it because to do so would require us to do something about it and that would involve change? I can assure you that our children already know that something "feels off." Hence, just one of the reasons why our educational system is falling apart.

When we let go of our arrogance, that we are the mightiest power that ever existed, we open windows and doors of opportunity. Something else to think about: In what other areas, such as: economics, government, finance, education, religion, etc. can we, the human race, be holding back our evolution, all due to EGO or the unwillingness to step outside our comfort zone?

It bears repeating that once you know something, you cannot "un-know" it. You can try, but what you are doing is having a foot in one reality (your mind) and the other in another reality (your heart - what you now know is your truth). When this happens, you literally pull yourself apart. The result is depression, anxiety and the illusion of fear.

Stretching your mind by exploring the unexplained is an adrenaline rush without substance abuse, or other types of addictions, such as: drugs, food, alcohol, sugar, caffeine, gossip, power, attention, etc. It shakes the very core of what we believe or think we already know. This is where personal and spiritual growth will begin with incredible momentum, resulting in much happiness, due to evolving into a much higher vibrational version of our self.

Why don't more people make an effort to explore the unexplained? It is simply because it is not comfortable. However, the important thing to remember is that when we stay in our comfort zone, we don't grow as a person or as a collective society. We then look outside of ourselves for things to make us feel better, which in turn, creates division by trying to compete with others for what we perceive to be a lack of physical or emotional resources.-

To illustrate another example: Did you know that dogs are not able to see all colors? Humans know that many different colors exist because our eyes are biologically able to see them. Even the human eye can only see a small segment of the electromagnetic light spectrum. There are also infrared, ultraviolet, microwave, x-rays, radio waves, gamma rays, and likely other light waves, that we are not aware even exist, because our modern technology is not yet capable of detecting them. Therefore, could it also be possible that other things may exist that we cannot biologically see? Some of it has yet to be discovered. Could we be so arrogant as to think that we are the highest evolved species ever created in the billions of years this planet has existed?

What if we were to open our minds to the possibility that there is so much more going on here on our physical planet than we would have ever guessed or been taught? There IS more happening right now in this time and space than we could possibly imagine. In fact, the human brain has been programmed by outside influences not to imagine it at all. That is why we cannot see it, at least not until we train our brain to be open to it.

Historians have said that when Columbus discovered America, the Indians who lived here could not see his ships on the horizon of the ocean, because they had never before seen anything like it. Their limited minds could not grasp the possibilities. Interesting, don't you think? The Indians didn't see them coming, because they could not fathom such a thing as a ship!

Ants cannot fathom simple math with their limited awareness. We know it exists and understand it. If ants could think, and who knows that they can't, they could be thinking that their world is as big as their little anthill, or a certain radius around the anthill. However, our human minds know that much more exists than the ant can imagine.

In fact, there may be infinite galaxies that are similar to our galaxy. However, our EGO would have us believe that we are the center of the universe. EGO keeps us from experiencing all of reality as it is meant to be. Imagine what we would be able to create, if collectively, we opened up our minds and hearts. Instead, we often hoard what we know, and argue about who owns it and who is right. Next, we look outside of ourselves to gather like-minded people who agree with our limited perspective. In this way, we feel more confident in continually beating the drum of proving other groups wrong. Wouldn't our time be better invested by focusing on co-creating through the process of co-operation rather than division? Can you see how much more we could possibly be doing for the people of this planet and Mother Earth as well?

Ask yourself these questions and be very honest with your answers. Why am I here? What could possibly be the purpose of humanity's existence? You can be sure that it is not to hurt, fight with, or kill each other. The purpose is as unique for each individual person, as our fingerprints and DNA. Our mission is to help each other, just like the limbs, twigs, and leaves of a tree work together in co-operation to help the entire tree to thrive.

Throughout history, the societies that thrived for the longest periods of time were those that realized that cooperation was the key to a thriving community, rather than aggression and competition. Even when we call it "healthy competition" in order to externally motivate one's self and others to do better, we are always creating division. When this happens, it devalues someone. All branches of the same tree are just as important as the others to help in sustaining life.

Once we understand that when we look inside ourselves, we will realize that we are okay just the way we are, and we know we already have everything we need. We have always had it. It only requires opening our hearts to ourselves and other people. This is because we are all connected. We are all one, and everything that affects one of us, affects the whole. Everything that infects one can also infect the whole. Which type of world would you choose to live in?

Returning to the tree metaphor, if a branch is cut off of a tree, it affects the entire tree. Apply this analogy to the human race. We annihilate and bomb other countries, because we judge them to be wrong based on a specific standard and culture that we say is the only "right" way to live. Could they be defending themselves and their culture from what they consider to be overly aggressive, power-hungry people? Again, some cultures see aggressiveness, competition, greed, and the overpowering of others as a mental illness.

Our actions create our world, therefore, every single person is responsible, individually, and collectively, for the world we live in right now. It has always been our choice how we create by the choices we make.

The great news is we are all able to make a change. We can make a pivotal shift right now. That is what the year 2012 was all about. The 2012 dooms-day rumors were never about the destruction of the world. It referred to a time shift in our conscious awareness of how we affect each other, the planet, and our solar system. This was a shift in frequency of vibration, so that we all begin to become more attentive, aware, and involved. When we are able to affect and motivate enough people to make that shift, it WILL change the world as we know it, for the better. It will raise our consciousness and empower us to look beyond ourselves. We will then realize we are all one with each other and with nature. Yet, at the same time, we will know that our answers to life's greatest questions are found within.

The question is: Will we allow our EGOs to hold us back? When we hold ourselves back, we hold back many others who we could potentially influence and together create a better world for the greater good of all.

Every single human being on our planet has a choice to make. A) We can be on the defensive, compete, accuse others, fight, and annihilate each other; all because we feel there is not enough power, money, health, and success to go around. B) Create a world where everyone wins and stress is greatly reduced or no longer exists. There is enough of everything for everyone and we can all make it our business to see that everyone's needs are met. It takes sharing to a whole new level.

It doesn't take a lot of people to make a shift. Once you get any number of innovative visionaries willing to come together with Divine Intention, it raises the frequency of the planet. When that happens, the rest will join in, especially when they begin to see positive results. Time and time again, it has been proven that when a pivotal point occurs (or what many refer to as a "paradigm shift") it is adopted by mainstream as socially acceptable.

Dr. David Hawkins refers to this paradigm shift process as counterbalancing the weakness of the masses, using a scale referred to as "the level of consciousness." In summary, what this means is that it only takes a small group of people in a high-frequency heart coherent state to create a massive paradigm shift in any area of life.

The next question is, are you willing to join me and many others in immediately replacing those dysfunctional, but socially acceptable activities that are not serving us? For example, let's start with some of the obvious: power addictions, overeating, junk food, substance abuse, criticizing others for entertainment, negative self talk, and competing with each other? When we make those activities not acceptable for a society that wants to evolve into a higher level of consciousness, we then make co-operation acceptable by the general population. If we don't make that shift, we are basically cutting off our branches, and our tree will actually end up dying.

Let's be careful about not confusing the process of raising our electromagnet frequency, with the 1960's "hippy movement." It was commonly referred to as the Age of Aquarius, made famous by the popular song of the era. This confusion is usually among the group of people who do not really understand astrology. Some of those who may actually have believed in the principles of the hippy culture or movement, became more caught up in the trappings of the times, rather than it's purpose.

However, that is the result when minds and hearts are not fully open to exploring the things that are not understood. When this occurs, those people are missing out on a tremendous amount of information that will shift their world into a place that they can only imagine. Meanwhile, if they are in a position of power or influence over others, they hold back everyone that has become dependent on them.

On the date of September 11, 2001, scientific proof was recorded and documented, that our satellite systems picked up a dramatic increase of electromagnetic frequency from the planet's activity of human emotions. I think we all remember in our hearts what occurred on that date.

Rather than attempt to explain this scientific documentation, below is a link to The Global Coherence Initiative where you will find the documentation and illustrations of the stress wave that is thought to be caused by mass human emotion. This is believed to have created modulations in the geomagnetic field of the earth within 15 minutes of the first plane hitting the first Twin Tower in New York City. Can we, with all our hearts, still dispute that human emotion is not important or does not have some effect on everything? www.glcoherence.org

Gregg Braden, a world-renowned author on the subject of connecting to your heart, and a big advocate of HeartMath® (www.heartmath.org) and of the Global Coherence Initiative (www.glcoherence.org), speaks about this incident in his books and presentations. He has the ability to draw the attention of both men and women, like a powerful magnet, when he connects his heart to the audience.

Science now knows and has proven that everything is energy and has a specific vibration. Everything is alive. They have begun to accept that each person, animal, object, planet, in fact, **everything** has a magnetic field. This magnetic field is sometimes referred to in what mainstream calls New Age literature as an "aura."

While scientific information about our brain and its capacity is limited, we do know that most people only use a small percentage of it.

Some think that the brain is the source of the magnetic field. However, once again, it has been scientifically proven that the heart has a much stronger magnetic field than the brain. The heart is the first organ formed in the mother's womb when a baby is conceived. With that knowledge, it makes sense that the heart is not only the space in which we want to be, but also the place in which we want to live our lives.

The HeartMath® Institute has developed a personal hand-held device called the emWave®. This little devise is something that you can buy at a reasonable price and monitor your own heart coherence. It lets you know without judgment whether you are in your head, moderately in your heart, or completely in your heart, at any given time. This device can be used when you are on the phone, whether with a client or a friend in need of your advice. They won't know you are using it, but they will notice a big difference in you. It assists you in learning to listen from the heart (not the head or ears). With the feedback from this little device monitoring your heart space, you can instantly re-adjust your focus. They will be magnetically attracted to you because they know you are in your heart with them, instead of just hearing them.

We know that hearing is a biological response to sound coming into our ears. Connecting with people through our heart means really listening and understanding, as well as empathically connecting at a soul level.

People are magnetically attracted to others who are in their heart space. The emWave® will help you to train yourself over time, so that even when it is not attached to you, you will know at any given moment whether you are in your head or your heart. It is also the perfect way to show that someone who is energetic, perpetually busy, and easily excited, isn't necessarily in heart coherence.

While writing this book and all future volumes, it was important to me to be in heart coherence as much as possible. It was not an easy task but with the help of HeartMath® technology, I am happy to report this book was written from what I call Divine Intention using the emWave® technology. I do hope that you feel this frequency as you read it.

There are people such as Mohandas Karamchand Gandhi and Mother Theresa, who have been in their heart space often. They trained themselves to do that whether they were consciously aware of it or not. How they felt was more important to them than anything else. When they were in alignment and feeling good within their heart space, it was a magnetic attraction that helped others be in the same space. That is where we all want to be. The heart space is where joy, happiness, love, peace, security, and safety reside. It is nowhere outside of us, but is always within us.

Your Afterlife Reality: It's a Choice!

Scientific studies on the human brain now indicate that our thoughts create our current reality. We can choose to think differently about any situation at any given time and it will literally change what we experience. The power of choosing our own thoughts intentionally is the only thing that we **can** control.

Since we know our thoughts create our reality, what kind of afterlife reality do you want to create for yourself?

With this knowledge, that which you think will happen after death could be your exact experience, because your thoughts now and then may create it. Therefore, regardless of your religious/spiritual beliefs, wouldn't our ability to choose also be an infinite cycle, not only on this physical planet, but in the afterlife as well?

Let's use the metaphor of the clothing we put on every morning in relation to how we show up in the world. The emotions we put on will affect not only how our day goes, but also other people. What kind of person will you be today? How we think will be exactly what we will experience, not only in this lifetime, but also in an infinite number of lifetimes. Isn't it great to know that we get an infinite number of chances to evolve with joy into BEing spiritually intelligent?

Recycled Light & You

As was mentioned in a previous chapter, everything is infinite. There is no limit to what we can accomplish. There is no limitation on finances. There is no limitation or scarcity of power or resources. Limitations are merely illusions; this is because everything changes form eventually. Everything in life has it's cycle: seasons, earth's rotation around the sun, moon's rotation around the earth, planet alignment in the solar system, etc. Even this book is a cycle and a circle in motion, with some principles stated several times in different ways as they are inter-related to other topics. It is important to note that the human mind often must see and hear things a number of times before the heart feels it. When the student is ready the teacher appears. Sometimes the teacher is a book.

Our lives are a cycle too. Where are repeated patterns showing up in our lives? We've heard it many times before that history repeats itself. Why then, do we continue to limit ourselves by refusing to consider that our spirit/soul is also in it's own cycle? Many people believe that when we die, we go into black nothingness. Lights out. We are gone. That is fine, if that is what they wish to experience. We are all on the path of our own choosing. There is no wrong way when it serves us.

Some believe that we go to a place where we will be punished for doing things in this life that we were told are bad, and that we stay there forever. They believe that if we were good in this life, we go to a place of beauty and wonder, because we are rewarded for being good.

Still others believe that because everything is a cycle, we get to choose to come back into any dimension, perhaps not on this physical planet. Or maybe on this physical planet as the same energy, a being of light dressed in another human biological body.

Why is it difficult to accept the term "reincarnation?" Honestly, I too, had closed my mind at times on this subject. This word has had so many negative connotations applied to it, and so much misinformation attached, that it frightens people.

People are often drastically opposed to things they do not understand, or are unwilling to become educated about it. Sometimes it is because they don't want to understand another's perspective. It makes them angry, fearful, and often defensive. Still others find their peace and are grounded by it.

For those who do not like the term "reincarnation," let's use my preferred, and I believe, a more accurate description, "Energy Recycling." To better understand, open your mind and look around. Realize that everything is in motion. Everything is connected energy. Everything is needed to support the whole for it to be at its best. Would it make sense then, that it is the same with the recycling of our soul, which is also energy in motion in the form of light? When you know and accept this on the deepest level, the fear of death no longer exists.

You may have or know someone who has had a near death experience. In fact, it is becoming so commonplace that the medical community can no longer ignore it nor deny it occurs. While there are some variations, the majority of people who have NDEs (Near Death Experiences) have said that they see and feel their spirit/soul float out of their body. Similarly, they see a bright beautiful light and experience intense emotions of love and peace and that it is truly indescribable in human words.

Side Note: There are those words, "feel" and "emotion" again. Isn't it interesting that they keep showing up? Why then do we make our emotions wrong or ignore them? They are there to guide us to know more fully what we want, and what is or is not best for us at any given moment. The most emotionally intelligent people I know are the most grounded and forward focused, yet have a non-ego magnetic attraction about them. They are compassionate and accepting of everyone and everything and fully confident in what they know to be true for them. Life for them is lived in authenticity by following their heart without hidden or manipulative agendas.

A Time Shift

Here is an example of how everything is connected. According to Discovery.com the smallest particles that we know about are fermions, hadrons, and bosons. These particles are connected to subatomic particles more commonly known as protons, neutrons, and electrons. Protons, neutrons, and electrons are connected to atoms. Atoms are connected to molecules. Molecules are connected to solid items like trees, clouds, your office desk - everything. These solid items are connected in our world, as we are connected to Mother Earth. Mother Earth is connected to the solar system, without which, she could not survive, and vice versa. Because everything and everyone is connected, our very survival depends on how well the other flourishes.

Scientists now know that there are an infinite number of galaxies. Consider then, that the same must be true for things that are infinitely smaller. As previously stated, an ant sees it's little world as all there is. Because we are much bigger than an ant, from our perspective, we believe we are much more intellectually evolved and therefore, more knowledgeable.

Are we as humans taking the same perspective as the ant in thinking this is all there is? Like the ant, we are limiting our beliefs and our thinking to what we can see with the naked eye, or that which science says is so. Are we bordering on arrogance to assume that we are all there is or could be?

What will it take to create a shift in our current mindset? In the last few years, there had been a trend in movies, books, and on talk shows of predicting the physical destruction of Mother Earth on December 21, 2012. Unfortunately, the media had a hand in the propaganda that frightened some people into believing that the earth would be eliminated, or at least that most of it's population would be annihilated, just like the Y2K scare. There were a lot of speculations, predictions, and many theories from various cultures across the planet.

Allow me to share what I have observed in myself and in others. Though you may not have consciously been aware of it, I am sure you too, have experienced it to some degree.

Have you noticed that time is speeding up? Our days are going by faster than ever before. There is sometimes a subtle, but intense surge of energy. (I am not referring to hyperactivity, by any means. Increased energy flow has nothing to do with hyperactivity or how excited someone appears.)

Furthermore, this is different than anything in our past history. You may remember your grandparents saying that 'time flies', they 'just don't know where the time has gone,' or that 'the older they get the faster time goes', etc. Many of us have not only noticed this phenomenon, but have experienced it, including myself. It is accelerating at a powerful rate in a different way than in the past. It has become more intense than ever before.

Some have described it as "time collapsing on itself." What does that look or feel like? When you consider that everything is happening all at once: past, present, and future, is it safe to assume that we are being given a glimpse of it right now? It is called a "time shift."

Those who have become aware of this intense energy surge realize that this "time shift" is necessary to "change everything" as we know it. It is clear that this process is already well under way.

As we are all aware, every one of our current infrastructures that are in place is falling apart to one degree or another. We are witness to the medical field's failing health systems, the economy, personal and corporate finance, not to mention the political system in most of the world.

The upside of this is that it is causing people to not only rethink, but to restructure how they are living and define what is most important to them. Remember, the more we resist something we know we have to do, the more it will continue to nudge us harder and harder until we do it, thus creating a shift. Otherwise, it will "reboot" the system, in order for us to stay in balance, by creating a Divine matrix of situations that will challenge us to change immediately. Isn't it interesting that most people will make the necessary change, when something that they do not desire is about to happen or has just happened?

Here are some examples: More and more people are realizing that they have knowingly been eating unhealthy foods in large quantities. Some people have been intentionally voting for political and/or religious figures that do not align with their truth, simply because it's the popular thing to do.

There are people who spend erratically, living way beyond their financial means or sensible needs, because they think that the amount of their possessions equal their success, which they believe equates to their self-worth. Have they become addicted to the rush of emotions that they receive by acquiring expensive things? Is it because having these things makes them feel they have value and they want others to recognize and/or acknowledge their value by having them?

The one thing we CAN do to prepare ourselves for anything in the future is to become spiritually aware of our BEingness – our greatness. How are we showing up to others in our world? How are we connecting to other people? How are we treating others, especially those who are in opposition to us? Are we being competitive? Combative? Controlling? In contrast, are we living in our heart space? Are we finding a way to co-operate so that everyone not only has enough, but also is acknowledged for their importance on this planet - with no one left out?

When and if things get really tough for life as we know it, we will want and need to have already practiced treating people by The Golden Rule: "Do unto others as you would have them do unto you." It must become a way of life, instead of an occasional option.

What I found to be true in every case is that people who do not understand something and are unwilling to explore other people's perspectives, will have extreme and sometimes aggressive reactions because they are afraid. For many people, fear shows up as judgment.

How can you determine if you are judging someone and to what degree? Measure it by how far away your intention is from love, and how emotionally charged your thoughts are that create a re-action. Ask yourself why you are feeling this way. When you get the answer, again ask yourself, "Is this true or a distortion to justify my re-action to protect my ego?"

You can detach from an emotional charge and simply notice something. It takes practice in grounding yourself and stepping away from judgment, which does not serve anyone. Judgment is really about our own lack of self-esteem and value at that very moment. It has little to do with the person being judged.

Unfortunately, it's more socially acceptable today to judge and abuse another in this way and label it as being "assertive" and "entertainment," rather than to simply say, "I don't understand. Will you help me understand?" or to just let the negative emotional charge go.

The best way to handle anything that is in direct opposition to our perspective is to do what Jesus would do. That is, to choose LOVE. Regardless of how someone re-acts, any intense negative re-action is based on FEAR, and not knowing how to let go of it. BEing Spiritually Intelligent is about not having to make someone wrong or have power over them in order to feel worthy or have value.

What would happen if we were all to look at the time shift we are experiencing as being a positive series of events that will make the world a better place to live for the greater good of all? Let us consciously rethink the answers to the following questions:

- Who are we?
- How are we treating our bodies?
- How are we treating our finances?
- How are we treating our planet?
- How are we treating each other?
- Are we involved in a belief system that comes from a place of LOVE for everyone; that teaches, encourages co-operation, and co-creation, rather than division?

Be grateful for those with different perspectives. It is important that we have and respect opposite opinions, cultures and lifestyles, so that we know more clearly who we are, how we want to intentionally feel, and what we want to create in our lives. This doesn't make anyone wrong. It simply means that we can experience ourselves more fully when we see, feel, and know that something is not what we want. We must have the courage to BE authentic by staying on our own path without making others wrong.

For example: The colors, Caribbean Blue and Red Rock Orange, are currently my favorites. I cannot know these colors as my favorites, if I did not know that there were other colors to choose. Other colors are not wrong; but I can appreciate my favorite colors more because I know the other colors exist.

So with so much information on personal development, leadership development, and spiritual development, how do you know what to believe? Read on to discover a simple answer to this ongoing quest to dissolve the confusion.

❤ ❤ ❤

10

DO YOU BELIEVE
OR DO YOU KNOW?

There is a big difference between believing and knowing. There is also some misconception concerning the words "believe" and "know."

For example: When I say, "I believe my eyes are brown," or "I know my eyes are brown." Which statement sounds more confident to you?

Words are incredibly powerful. Words create and are created by our thoughts. Therefore, if I say, "I believe my eyes are brown," then there is an underlying implication to myself, and others, that I am not real sure. Perhaps I am having doubts that I was taught the color brown the same as everyone else.

However, if I say, "I know my eyes are brown" (in the light that the human eye can see), then I am making the statement that I am 100% sure that I know the color brown. I am leaving it open to the fact that I also know the human eye can only see a small spectrum of colors.

The same is true if we say, "I believe I will create an extra $5,000 by the end of the summer," or "I know I will create an extra $5,000 by the end of the summer."

Believing comes from the head. *Knowing comes from the heart.* When you know that you know that you know, nothing or no one can shake you from that knowingness. You cannot explain how you know; you just do. Understand that the "knowing" I am talking about has nothing to do with EGO or intellectual knowing.

Knowing is the heart space in which you want to BE, because words play a significant part in our life. When we "think" something, we are creating it. We make it far more real when we "say" it. Writing it down solidifies it further. When we share it with someone else, we really create momentum in what we are striving for, because one of two things will happen. People will either want to help us, or some will want to create the same things in their own lives. This is another way in which we teach. As a team with like-interests we are far stronger, that is, as long as all the team members have the same Divine Intention. We are stronger because we are raising the group's collective consciousness and vibrational frequency. Again, their intention and their mission, is to create in a manner that will produce a win-win situation for all.

Furthermore, remember that trust is the most important component that determines the momentum and longevity of any relationship. This certainly applies even in business where the true brand is "trust." It is the emotion that bonds the heart connection. Any long-term successful business will want to adopt this as their main focus and mission. Without trust any other vision of a mission is short lived. Trust is the bridge, the catalyst to a strong bond in every personal or business relationship.

When there is no trust, we create dis-trust, which creates dis-ease, which creates physical disease. This can quickly go viral in the opposite direction through the body and through an organization, which is the opposite of where you want it to go, *unless it isn't*.

When distrust repeatedly occurs, it is an urgent wake up "call to action," to create a pivotal point that will turn it around quickly. How quickly, depends on the willingness to co-create and the co-operation of all parties involved. This means letting go of the EGO and looking at the situation for the greater good of everyone.

It may not be surprising that some people thrive on creating dysfunctional situations through the only low-frequency techniques that they currently know, such as: intimidation, humiliation, manipulation, and isolation. It is because this is the only way they know how to survive at this point in their life.

That doesn't mean you have to play the game, nor be insulted by what they don't yet know. Step into BEing the natural leader in a Divine League of Visionaries. BE Spiritually Intelligent and take personal response-ability from a soul level. You want to come from a place that goes beyond game playing intellect. A good life isn't about outsmarting and/or outlasting. Deep within, everyone desires a coherent and co-operative lifestyle. This comes from the heart, not the head. Many don't know how to get there without bulldozing their way through. That's okay. When you set the example, they eventually will, *unless they don't*. If they choose not to, it is not your job to convince them otherwise. They have full response-ability for what they create. What they will create will be based on the energy frequency where they currently are, which will in turn, will attract like energy. However, it depends on his or her willingness to reach for and choose a higher frequency that will allow everyone to win.

The best advise is to follow what your heart is telling you. Your heart knows that annihilating someone, creating angst, attempting to ruin someone's reputation, or attacking someone's character, is not the way to resolve any issue. Those are old school, early 1900's tactics. As a society, it is imperative that we evolve into the realm of co-operation. Most of us learned these unattractive tactics as early as grade school, if not before. Some are still stuck there, because they just do not know any other way - yet. However, what they know or do not know is NOT at all your concern. Your foremost concern is you. When you are your best at any given moment, you lift others by being an example of Divine Love that is unshakeable from your core BEingness.

It's been said by many a learned master, that character is doing the right thing, even when others are not looking. Do the right thing because YOU know it is the right thing to do. It does not matter whether others know it, are watching, or not. What is important is that you know what has happened, how you re-acted to it, and whether you chose to look at the positive or the negative.

Here is another exercise for you: Since believing is different than knowing, I would suggest that from this moment forward, every time you think of using the words "believe" or "belief," change it to "know, knowing, or knowingness." You will immediately know intuitively, whether or not that statement is true for you. If it isn't true for you, find out why it is not. That is the process of questioning yourself to discover the WHY behind the WHY. What is your overall true intention for any statement?

Here are examples of intentions that do not serve everyone because they do not create a win-win environment:

- Beating someone. (Competing for the win is a scarcity mentality. There is enough to go around so that everyone feels they won.)
- Keeping up with the Jones. (So as to feel worthy and valued.)
- Being the all-powerful one (So others recognize you as being great, or great at what you do. This is a lack of confidence in your spiritual intelligence that shows up as EGO. Everyone is powerful and brings greatness to society.)

Always attempt to identify the win-win for everyone involved, including people who are not yet involved, but will eventually be affected or influenced in the future. Practice this even if it is only in the slightest way - by simply observing and feeling your energy frequency and that of others.

❤ ❤ ❤

11

GRATITUDE & APPRECIATION

The words and practice of gratitude and appreciation are valuable to our well-BEing. Our words can be our friend or they can work against us. It is our choice how we use them, and the outcome of their use is always based on our intention.

There is a simple exercise that I would suggest you do now to help keep you grounded, and at the same time stay in your heart space. First, be aware that it is normal for our human ego to attempt to get in the way of doing this exercise:

Every day for the next three days, every hour on the hour while you are awake, sit for 30-60 seconds, breathe deeply and notice what has occurred in the last hour that you really appreciate. It may be as simple as the gas station attendant being really polite to you. Perhaps your spouse helped clean up the dinner dishes. Maybe it was someone who cordially allowed you to go first, when you both arrived at a four-way stop at the same time.

Then, for the next three days, every hour on the hour while you are awake, articulate your appreciation in words by speaking it out loud – not just thinking it – for 30-60 seconds. If you are in a public place, you can still do this exercise in a low whisper, as if you were talking to yourself. Everyone already talks to themselves, in their head or out loud, and often both; you may as well make it enjoyable!

Finally, for three more days, every hour on the hour while you are awake, increase the time to 2-3 minutes. You will reach the point that everything you see, you appreciate, and you will begin to see everything from a new perspective. You will begin to see beyond the obvious.

For example, if you look at a piece of art, say a hand crafted glass vase, there are many things to see, imagine, and appreciate, besides a simple container for flowers and water. Such as:

- What was the craft person who created it like?
- What was their inspiration?
- Truly see the colors and how they swirl into shapes and designs that look differently from each angle.
- Envision and appreciate the loving care that went into crafting the piece.

- Envision and appreciate the process by which it arrived in the place where it is now so you have the opportunity to appreciate its beauty.
- See how it is sitting on the table and wonder about the person that put it there.
- What were they thinking when they placed it there and what were they hoping to create?
- See the table it is on and the other objects around it in relationship to the vase.
- Which other types of flowers would look lovely in the vase?

Understand then, that it is not just a vase. There were many actions taken by many people to get it there. Appreciate everyone who had a hand in putting it in front of your eyes to admire.

This is the heart space where we can all go without mind-altering substances, beverages, or food. We have the ability to access it at any time by simply going deeper with our appreciation and gratitude. Practice this exercise. Doesn't it feel better than obsessing over what you don't like? Feel the difference between the two emotions. The great news is that this exercise will raise your energetic vibrational frequency.

No matter what example is used, this exercise works when you come from a place of true Divine Intention for the greater good. It will not work if you doubt it or come from a place of greed, or self-expectations that will benefit only self or a group of people.

In case it has crossed your mind that I am out of MY mind, yes "in deed," BEing out of the mind is where you will want to BE when you do this exercise.

Did you catch the play on words used in this book? "Indeed" vs. "In Deed?" The word "indeed" may feel like I'm trying to convince you or put more emphasis on the fact that I know I am "indeed" out of my mind. When I come from a place of "In Deed," I come from a place of looking at things from a broader perspective. I am In Deed of service to others by BEing within my heart. When I raise my frequency and in a place of Divine Intention, I am always of service to others in ways I may never know. So are you!

The process is about appreciating and expressing gratitude from the heart which will bring you a positive and lasting result. This means not just reciting a memorized script from the mind (which holds our memories). This may actually move things farther away from you.

All spiritual teachers, myself included, will acknowledge that we are human and sometimes our human side emerges. However, the more practice you give it, the easier it becomes, and the more grounded you are in your knowingness. Thus, the clearer you will become about who you really are.

When you know who you are and live in your authenticity, all of the things that used to bug you, and that you allowed to ruin your day, fall away and are now of little significance. This doesn't mean that you won't notice them; you just do not allow them to defuse your focus. You discover that it is no longer important to hold onto things that do not express who you really are, nor do you allow someone to attempt to pull you into their issues. You are designing a new life, a new way of BEing, and that life is created around what matters the absolute most to you. Ultimately, you will discover that it is and always has been about what matters most to you: how you feel.

This is not selfishness. How we feel can affect how others feel. When we are not feeling good emotionally, physically, mentally or spiritually, other people are affected by our low frequency energy. Unless they are highly grounded and have a clear picture of who they are at all times, they will feel this negativity to one degree or another. It is their personal response-ability to learn to lovingly, but with graceful assertion, deal with energies coming toward them that do not match their frequency. To be selfish would be to put everyone and everything else ahead of your own emotions. It is "In Deed" the exact opposite of what most of us have learned.

What's the Next Step?

Now that you know who you are and who you were meant to BE, are you wondering about the next step? Volume II explains: How to KNOW you are on your own unique authentic path, and what to you do with that information to create a higher evolved self and life.

12

LOVE, LIGHT & NAMASTE

When you have any kind of communication with me, through email, snail mail, Facebook, other social media venues, or one of my workshops, you will hear me use the words, "Love, Light and Namaste" separately or together. It is important that you understand what these words mean to me when I use them.

When you contact me, I pledge that I will respond with grace and kindness. That is why it is so important that you know what I mean by these words. When coming from a place of Divine Intention, know that a few words are all that is needed to express my heart space of BEing with you, seeing you, and connecting with your energy, thus lifting you up:

Love - Love is the one and only emotion. Everything else is based on fear. Humans have created fear as a mechanism for control. It never was nor will it ever be, who you are. I recognize you as Love(d).

Light - Continuously remind yourself, until you truly know beyond a shadow of a doubt, we are all pure white vessels of light; that is, spiritual beings of light energy that reside in a human biological form. The body is our costume, our shell. We are goodness and grace and whole. When I send Light, I send pure positive energy that will lift you up. This we can do unto and for each other every day.

Namaste -
I honor you.
I respect you.
I see who you really are.
I see your greatness.
I honor your greatness.
I will not judge.
I will not make you wrong.
I will lift you up to see and feel the BEing that you really are.
I will allow you to BE who you really are.
I see you as Love(d), always and in all ways.
Namaste.

❤ ❤ ❤

LIGHTBABIES

We are Lightbabies. Golden Grace.
Wings, meant to fly.
We are delicate and pregnant with goodness.
We are each made of such a quiet that the entire
Universe can hear us.
There is only the Unfolding; the Opening ever
happening.
All else are thoughts – lollipops for the mind.
We … are *Lightbabies* parading as Humankind.

~Em Claire from her book of beautifully
radiant poems,
"Silent Sacred Holy Deepening Heart"
www.emclairepoet.com

ABOUT THE AUTHOR

Susan Abrams Milligan is an author, personal development and spiritual coach. She is also a certified health coach and trains other health coaches. She has helped

SUSAN ABRAMS MILLIGAN

many people re-discover who they really are as well as become successful entrepreneurs.

Her desire to share her insight into these principle truths is due to her deep personal experience in self-discovery and in manifesting her desires. She has an internal passion for helping others to change their own lives by creating the next highest version of who they really are.

From her small town mid-western roots, to the beautiful landscapes of the desert southwest, she enjoys living with goodness and grace and always re-creating a higher version of herself through the expression of LIFE.

She and her husband, Michael, make their home in Sedona, Arizona, along with their Cairn Terriers, Molly May and Happy Jack and their feline friend, Little Cat.

"The Missing Link Between Who You Are & Who You Were Meant to BE" is Volume I of the *BEing Spiritually Intelligent* series.

To learn more about the other volumes in the series, visit the series' website:

www.beingspirituallyintelligent.com

Susan's author website and blog:
www.susanabramsmilligan.com

You can also find Susan on various social media networks.

❤❤❤

This Volume was created with ❤ and ☼ in Sedona, Arizona

RECOMMENDED RESOURCES

I would highly recommend any books, services or media by the following spiritual teachers. Visit their websites for additional information:

Neale Donald Walsch
Em Clair
Dr. Robert Holden
Dr. Wayne Dyer
Louise L. Hay
Cheryl Richardson
Dr. Joe Dispenza
Eckert Tolle
Byron Katie
Napolean Hill
Marianne Williamson
Caroline Myss
Gregg Braden
Dr. David Hawkins
Esther & Jerry Hicks (Abraham)
Shakti Gawain
James Redfield
Marcia Wiener
Alan Cohen
Brian Johnson
John Holland
Ram Dass
Koelle Simpson

Other books:

- "A Course in Miracles" by The Foundation for Inner Peace
- "The Hidden Messages in Water" by Masaru Emoto
- "The Power of Flow" by Charlene Belitz and Meg Lundstrom
- "When God Winks" by Squire Rushnell

Other Websites & Resources:

Greatness Button Challenge: www.shareyourgreatness.com

AHHH Lifestyle: www.ahhhlifestyle.com

Law of Knowing: www.lawofknowing.com

HeartMath® Institute: www.heartmath.com

Hay House: www.hayhouse.com

Klemmer & Associates: www.klemmer.com

Mishka Productions: www.mishka.com

Earthing: www.earthing.com

emWave & emWave 2: www.heartmath.com

Omega Institute:
www.eomega.org
Holosync by Centerpointe Institute:
www.centerpointe.com
"I Am" (documentary) by Tom Shadyac:
www.iamthedoc.com
"What the Bleep Do We Know" (documentary):
www.whatthebleep.com
"Thrive" (documentary) by Foster Gamble:
www.thrivemovement.com
"The Dash" (Poem) by Linda Ellis:
www.lindaellis.net

Visit the book series' website where you will find
other resources and links:
www.beingspirituallyintelligent.com

Author's website and blog:
www.susanabramsmilligan.com

❤ ❤ ❤

NOTES

NOTES

www.ingramcontent.com/pod-product-compliance
Lightning Source LLC
LaVergne TN
LVHW021446080426
835509LV00018B/2183